MW00799366

JOURNEY TO CREATION

AWAKENING HUMANITY'S DESTINY

By
Wanda Zum-Mallen

COPYRIGHT

All rights reserved. No part of this book may be used or reproduced by any mechanical, photographic, or electronic process, or in the form of phonographic recording; nor may it be stored in a retrieval system, transmitted, or otherwise be copied for public or private use other than for "fair use" as brief quotations embodied in articles and reviews without prior written permission of the publisher.

The author of this book does not dispense medical advice or prescribe the use of any techniques as a form of treatment for physical, mental or medical problems without the advice of a physician or qualified psychotherapist, either directly or indirectly. The intent of this author is only to offer information of a general nature to help you in your quest for emotional and spiritual well-being. In the event you use any of the information in this book for yourself, which is your constitutional right, the author/publisher assumes no responsibility for your actions.

FIRST EDITION 2012
Copyright ©2012 Wanda Zum-Mallen
All rights reserved.
ISBN: 0985066202
ISBN 13: 9780985066208
Library of Congress Control Number: 2012912216
Wanda Zum-Mallen, Sedona, AZ

Cover Design by WANDA ZUM-MALLEN
Cover Photo: Dreamtime #ID17401641
SAVE THE EARTH by iGoRZH
Editing by DIAN CRYSTAL

Library of congress Cataloging-in-Publication Data
ZUM-MALLEN, WANDA, 1959-
JOURNEY TO CREATION/
BY WANDA ZUM-MALLEN
ISBN#978-0-9850662-0-8
    1. Creation. 2. God. 3. Soul. 4. Spiritual.

ACKNOWLEDGEMENTS

I would like to express my gratitude to Dian whose support through the years and out of this world editing made my dream a written reality. To all my friends and clients who believed in my gift and let me share it with them. To my family who gave me strength. And a special thank you to Creation for showing me the way home.

CONTENTS

∾

FORWARD

When I decided to write this book my intent was to share a true story from my younger days when I worked as a simple janitor and searched for my destiny. Instead of exploring the normal career world, such as college or tech school, I looked inside of myself. This deep, inner quest led me to reconnect to my soul and undergo an incredible journey through this universe and out to Creation. Upon arrival I was welcomed into an infinite light that gently surrounded me and permeated my being with an eternal love. Then a benevolent intelligence within this boundless light opened my perception with its wisdom and showed me how everything was created. It also revealed to me how each soul in every universe participated in the initial act of Creation.

While I moved deeper into this light, its strength reactivated an unlimited energy within the molecules of my being and I reconnected to the expansive life force within infinity. I knew I could explode and expand out in every direction to become every photon of Creation.

From this vast viewpoint I looked back at the world I lived in and changed my perspective. The infinite knowledge I had attained in Creation gave me the insight to understand that I came to earth to experience the exquisite pleasure of good and bad in a dimension of opposites or duality. The good I had taken inside my body and it validated my soul while the bad saturated my cells with heavy, crystalline forms of energy shutting down my life force. Its weight had taken over my mind and emotions impacting my body in a negative way. It consumed me and I was led to believe that I was a spirit imprisoned inside a body full of programs, belief systems, structures, limitations, traumas, pain, suffering and illness. On top of all of this, I realized the memory of my true identity had been wiped from my consciousness.

The saddest thing I became aware of was the lack of unconditional love in this dimension on earth. I had searched for true love but experienced conditional love. As a little girl, I heard if I was a good and did what I was told I would go to heaven. As I grew older my relationships were laced with desires, projections and contracts. My employers continued to perpetuate the illusion with the expectation of my perfect performance rewarded with greed. This web of delusion weaved its way through my life and trained me to accept limitations.

It slowly dawned on me that the answers lay inside my heart as well as each one of our hearts. I knew the ache and longing I felt and heard others talk about was our desire to remember our connection to our true home. I understood that the pain and suffering I felt and experienced with others developed compassion and bonding in our journey together. I became aware our amnesia was only temporary in this grand illusion.

When I returned from Creation, I changed my perception from being a small, unloved human on a great big earth spinning through a massive universe to a portal for the light of Creation. As the years went by I transformed my life and switched my focus to the powerful energy that flowed from the heavens into my heart and out my hands to manifest miracles. This fired up an inner light that illuminated my body and poured out of my eyes. This gave me a heightened sense of discernment to see through the illusion of this three dimensional world.

Decades after I experienced Creation and received my purpose, I began taking individuals to their soul and into Creation. Once they reconnected to this deep eternal love, they remembered their magnificent wisdom. They also accessed their benevolent power and let it flow into their lives which lifted them up into a heightened state of eternal energy that had no end and continuously renewed itself in every cell of their being. They returned with the full knowledge of their soul in their heart and how to accomplish their true purpose.

Then I began to guide groups to their soul and Creation; we searched together deep within our hearts and awakened to access the future. We saw there was more to us than our occupations or day-to-day lives and we reached above the limitations of this reality to fulfill our true destinies.

What you will read is a narrative of the events that took place that reawakened my soul's purpose. I was taken home to remember who I really am...now it is your turn to journey with me and let my story help you remember your soul, its destiny and your connection with Creation.

Chapter 1
SEARCH FOR MY DESTINY BEGINS

☙

My story begins in the summer of 1982, in the beautiful town of Monterey on the pristine coast of California. I was a tall, blue eyed blond with an athletic, twenty three year old body and a very stubborn Germanic spirit. Most people saw me as a tenacious tom boy, but in reality I was a shy, quiet introvert who dedicated herself to a life of hard work and very little social interaction. What they didn't know was under my strong, silent exterior was a tender heart that ached to know my true purpose in life and to fulfill it.

At the time, I lived a simple, but unusual life in an underground spa located within an up-scaled shopping mall called Del Monte Center. Manicured green lawns, ceanothus shrubs and rows of tiny purple and white alyssums graced the Macy's and Mervyns retail stores which stood like beacons in the center of the complex. Surrounding these monoliths were various shops providing all the extra necessities of life that beckoned the loyal patrons from miles around to indulge in a full day of retail therapy.

On the lower level was a large, underground parking garage for Macy's. Adjacent to that was a large outdoor courtyard surrounded with various clothing stores, a pizza parlor and a multi-screen movie theatre. Alongside the theatre was a long, covered corridor that seemed to lead to a dead end. Only those that wore colorful jogging suits and carried stylish gym bags were seen sprinting down to the end of this passageway. Then they disappeared behind two huge, mahogany doors which led them into the Del Monte Spa, an exclusive, a member's only playground.

These club members were greeted by a cheery receptionist who stood behind a highly polished, chest high wooden counter and behind this reception desk was painted a large rainbow that arched over the back wall continued down the hall. The guests signed their names on the register and headed down the hallway following the rainbow past two small offices and into the fitness room.

They entered this vast work out room to see numerous shiny Nautilus machines reflected in eight foot tall mirrors that lined the walls. Rows of shiny dumbbells sat poised on their racks like gold bars waiting for another day of strength training. In the back corner exercise mats were piled high on gold, shag carpeting that spread throughout the entire fitness room and into the offices. In contrast, each office was sparsely furnished with two thinly padded chairs and a dark brown, laminate desk with polished aluminum legs.

It was in this Nautilus room that my nightly routine began at ten in the evening. I was not a muscle bound personal trainer. I was the janitor and the janitor's closet was my locker. Seven days a week, I pulled out the window cleaner, super sized squeegee, and the industrial vacuum to start the tedious task of cleaning the tall mirrors and vacuuming the shag carpet. As I sprayed and wiped the oily finger prints from the mirror's reflective surface, I would catch an occasional glimpse of my face and notice the sadness in my eyes. It was as if I had become a self imposed prisoner and a slave to a job with no escape. My environment was luxurious and I had the keys to every door, but my perceptions and belief systems kept me a prisoner in this nightly, monotonous routine.

After cleaning the mirrors I focused on vacuuming the carpet in this outer chamber while my mind kept asking, "Why do I feel this way? What else can I do? Where can I go?"

The beater bar on the head of the vacuum made long, perfect furrows in the carpet giving it a groomed appearance. The questions I asked myself while I worked brought a deep ache and a longing from within my heart. I had to remember who I really was and what I was truly destined to do in my life.

After completing the outer chamber, I headed deeper underground into the inner chamber to clean the men's and women's locker rooms respectively. My back ached with pain as I scrubbed the greasy film off the rows of shower stalls and bathroom sinks. I moaned with anguish every time I scoured the rings out of the toilet bowls with a pumice stone or plunged the clogged toilets.

On the floor, long, thin brown mats lie between the benches and rows of lockers. These rubber mats had to be scrubbed, hosed down, rolled up and set upon the benches to dry. After hosing down the mats, I focused on the slick, yellow tile floor which was covered with an inch or two of gray water that coated my bare feet with hair and slime which clogged the drain. It smelled like sewage and it took a long time to scrub, drain and dry these floors.

Four hours of grueling work had gone by and I was beginning to feel sore from the lactic acid building up in my muscles along with the ache inside my heart. It was amazing how my physical and emotional pain could reach the same levels of intensity. I realized that being a janitor was not my life's work and I had to listen to this feeling deep within my heart that knew I had a special purpose.

No matter what I felt inside, I had to keep cleaning and finish my job. So after completing the locker rooms, I headed into the inner sanctum, the deepest underground chamber of the spa where the Jacuzzi, steam room, sauna, inhalation room and pool were a welcome sight. Surrounding the pool were tall, marble Greek statues that stood tucked in their private alcoves between the floor to ceiling pillars. Each one had a benevolent gaze that conveyed a wisdom that I had yet to understand or attain. Soft lights glowed from under the water and reflected off the statues creating a surreal environment.

When I entered this room at two in the morning, I would stop for a moment to pretend I was back at the healing pools of Rome. I imagined angels floating down pouring their divine energy into the pool. I slowly reached down and touched the warm water pretending to be healed of all my pain.

These moments of fantasy gave way to reality as I picked up the pool hose to vacuum out the debris. While the dirt slowly disappeared into the head of the vacuum from the bottom of the pool, I would often wonder how I could become like the gods. In my eyes they were elegant, benevolent and endowed with the knowledge and wisdom of the universes.

After I finished cleaning the pool I slowly made my way over to the earthy sauna. Its walls were made out of lava rock and lined with three rows of Redwood benches that retained the heat from the pile of lava rocks in the burner long after it had been shut off. As I scrubbed the benches the smell of the heated wood activated memories of sitting at a camp fire in the forest just outside Yosemite National Park. The thought of being free and out in nature released emotions deep in my heart which brought tears to my eyes. When I listened to those feelings in my heart that longed to know who I was and what I came here to do; I looked up at the ceiling, clenched my fists with rage and screamed in anguish through my clenched teeth, "I am not a slave!"

I could not understand what triggered these deep feelings, why I felt that way or what I was to do. Deep inside I felt like I was just beginning to wake up from amnesia.

These feelings followed me as I finished cleaning the sauna and walked next door to the bright, cheery, yellow tiled aromatherapy room where my nostrils filled with the smell of eucalyptus. I quickly scrubbed the tiles and squeegeed the windows. Next I moved into the large steam room where three tiered, white tile seats sat waiting for me to scrape and scrub a thick coating of body sweat and scum off their surfaces every night.

After six solid hours of grueling work and beating my mind to a pulp to uncover my real purpose in life, I decided it was time to look outside myself for help. I realized I would have to start asking for answers in the simple form of prayer. So I started praying while I worked. I would look up at the ceiling and in a strong voice I would say, "God, tell me my purpose!"

Actually what began as a simple prayer, turned into a demand and patience was not my virtue. Every hour my eyes turned upward and I cried out in agony aching for a reply. But my requests were always answered by a deafening silence no matter how many times I repeated them.

At four in the morning I completed my work, shut off all the lights, and fell exhausted to the floor in the office where I took my mid-work nap. The smelly carpet was cold and damp from the ocean fog, but it felt wonderful to lie down. I turned on the little room heater beside me to take the chill out of the air and told myself that the work kept my body strong and the prayers motivated me to believe that I would someday receive an answer. The gentle purring sound and warm air from the heater would comfort my mind, relax my body and slowly lullaby me to sleep.

Fifteen to thirty minutes later, I would be wide awake and ready to head up to the other side of the mall to complete the second portion of my job. As I walked out of the spa and locked those heavy mahogany doors behind me, I would look out into the large, empty parking lot with the lights casting a dim, fuzzy glow into the early morning air. The predawn atmosphere was eerie and usually filled with a thick, bone chilling London fog from the ocean which presented the perfect setting for a murder mystery. As I walked past the theatre I noticed it was dark and empty. Next door the pizza parlor reeked of beer and sour dough bread. I was usually very hungry at this time and the thought of wolfing down a calazone filled with cheese, peppers and pepperoni made my stomach growl. I hurried up the stairs, past Macys, Mervyns and along the corridors of shops towards my next destination.

My mind also raced with thoughts questioning my life, "How long could my body take this grueling work? Was I destined to lead my life as a slave?"

Then I would tell myself that if I was thinking these thoughts and questioning my existence there must be something inside of me that knew there was more to me. While my mind was noisy with its thoughts in those dark morning hours, I became aware that the businesses in this shopping complex were quiet and no one was around except the lazy security guards that occasionally patrolled the grounds.

My body relaxed a bit when I finally reached the spa annex on the other side of the mall. I placed my key in the lock of the oversized, dark wood French door and entered into a large exercise room. I opened the blinds that covered the entire front wall of floor to ceiling windows to let in the early morning sun that burned through the fog. The sides and back wall of this large room were lined with six foot mirrors which reflected the rays of light. A rich, blue carpet spread out before me and disappeared into two changing rooms in the back.

It only took a few minutes to clean the mirrors but the floor took longer. I dragged a smaller industrial sized vacuum out of the storage room, turned it on and began replacing the foot prints in the carpet with perfectly brushed rows while pleading with the forces of the heavens to just send an angel to tell me to go work with Mother Teresa and help the sick, dying and the poor. I repeated my prayer over and over begging for an answer. But no answer came. When I was done, I would unplug the vacuum and put it away in the back storage room.

It was after six in the morning and all I could think about now was sleep. I did not have to go far to my bed because it was located in the rafters above the ceiling in the storage room. To access it all I had to do was reach up and pull a rickety, wooden ladder down and crawl up into a spacious attic. The interior roof of this simple loft apartment looked like the inside of a hollow pyramid which was held up with massive laminated beams. Tension wires were suspended every two square feet from the roof to hold the metal framing for the ceiling above the aerobics room. Thin, white ceiling tiles lie nestled in the frames. They were very fragile and did not hold any weight. If I were to step on them they would split open and I would fall right through to the floor ten feet below.

I carefully crawled onto the center of the three, two by ten foot pieces of plywood which rested side by side on the metal framework of the ceiling. This is where my big, green sleeping bag lay with one stack of neatly folded clean clothes on one side and a dirty stack on the other. I gratefully unzipped my bag, slid inside my simple bed and closed my eyes to the world around me.

Within a few minutes I heard the aerobic instructor unlock the front door and turn on the stereo. Minutes later the class started and the music blasted while she yelled at the top of her lungs, "Now breath and stretch and lift and drop. Let's do it again with more gusto!" The boards vibrated and the rafters shook in tempo with the music. I felt like the Hunchback of Notre Dame high above civilization with the bells ringing in the belfry. These loud sounds were a welcome relief to my mental torment and they would comfort my body and lullaby me to sleep.

When the music stopped in the late evening, I woke up from the deafening silence and realize it was breakfast time. I quickly slipped into a clean pair of clothes and crawled down the ladder to begin my day. I ordered my food to go at the local deli or pizza parlor and took it to the park to share with the bossy blue jays and the hyperactive squirrels that gathered round me. It was fun to have their company and listen to them squawk and chirp in their own language till I threw them a morsel. I laughed as their polite requests turned into a free for all frenzy of feathers and bushy gray tails until one escaped with the fragment of food and disappeared into the forest.

My dinners with my wild friends usually ended much too quickly and I reluctantly left their company to begin my nightly job. Months went by and I kept working and praying while my techniques of asking for my purpose in life got really creative and demanding. Every night the gods watched as I commanded the angels to be present and give me a sign. Just a little ripple in the water would do. I even tried negotiating making deals and giving ultimatums. But, nothing ever happened. No answer. No response. Nothing physical or tangible that I could understand ever took place to give me an answer.

But I did not give up.

Chapter 2

FIRST OUT OF BODY EXPERIENCE

❦

The days and nights slowly passed and summer became winter. I kept asking for my purpose as spring arrived and the flowers began to bloom. Nine months had gone by and my prayers intensified to consume every waking moment of my life. To my surprise the answer finally came, but not in the way I had expected it to.

I finished my nightly routine at the spa around four in the morning, shut off all the lights, walked into the office to lie down on the floor and take a brief nap. My exhausted body relaxed and I became aware of the cold, damp moisture from the carpet so I turned on the heater. The warm air and the purring sound of the spinning fan comforted me and I fell instantly into a deep sleep.

I awoke from my nap a few seconds later and stood up. When I bent down to shut off the heater I realized I was standing next to my body. I was extremely confused and asked myself, "Am I dead?"

Then I stared at my body and noticed that it was breathing and my face looked very peaceful. I watched myself for a long time in shock expecting the eyes on my face to open and look at me, but they didn't. Then I looked down at my standing body and realized it looked the same as the one lying on the floor except it was translucent. It felt strong, vital, alive and powerful. It was invisible yet invincible. The authentic me that had jumped out of my skin was able to think with incredible clarity.

In the midst of trying to comprehend what was happening, I glanced into the Nautilus room and realized that the lights had been left on, but I remembered that I had just shut them off a few minutes ago. So, I turned and quickly walked out the office door to shut off the lights, but I wasn't walking, I was gliding. When that realization hit me, I lost my equilibrium for a moment and had to focus on maintaining my balance to stay upright. I cautiously continued to move forward and tried to avoid running into the Nautilus machines but my translucent body went right through them. A shock wave rippled through me with the awareness that I could move through anything and it wouldn't hurt because I was no longer made out of physical matter. As I floated towards the corner, I lost control and ended up taking a short cut through the wall and I was amazed I didn't get stuck. Next I tried to navigate around the rack of barbells in between the corner and the light switches but my ability to maneuver was awkward and I slid right through the rack. My translucent body felt the density of the barbells like ripples of invisible water moving through my legs. I was amazed they didn't stop me or effect my movement in any way.

I approached the light switches a little too fast and my body went too far, so I had to stop and back up to them. I put my arm up on top of the switch panel and with a downward motion tried to shut off the lights. My arm sank straight through to the back of the light panel and came out under the lower portion of it. A shiver went through my translucent body when the realization hit me that I didn't get electrocuted as I had expected. At the same time I was surprised when I saw that all the light switches were in their off positions. I was dumbfounded and wondered where the light was coming from.

My translucent arm still hung in the air as my eyes shifted from the panel of light switches to the light that filled the room. It was a radiant white, golden light and soft on the eyes, not harsh like the light from a fluorescent bulbs or the sun. It materialized out of thin air similar to white cumulus clouds forming in the atmosphere and it gently floated horizontally around the Nautilus room. It was quiet and filled the room with a strong sense of peace, love and tranquility that I had never experienced before.

Just by being in its presence I was spellbound and lulled into a blissful state of ecstasy. As I watched it drift around the room a thought occurred to me to ask it what my purpose was. So I floated over to it and with a strong voice from my luminescent vocal cords, I asked a simple question, "What is my purpose?"

I waited but no response came. The light floated silently around the room attempting to suck me in and carry me away. But I did not trust it. Again I asked, "please tell me what my real calling in life is?'

Again, no answer came. The light continued to float around the room and I felt drawn to it like a magnet. I though to myself, "If you are not going to talk to me then I am just going to stand here and watch you."

My mind was busy analyzing this light and I asked again, "What did I come to this earth to do?"

No answer. By now I was getting very frustrated and angry. I yelled, "I asked you a simple question and I deserve a simple answer."

It didn't matter how demanding I was or what I asked there was no response from this light that came from an unknown place. It just kept floating around the room in a casual, peaceful manner as if it was taunting me to investigate its source. Eventually I got so frustrated I gave up and decided to go back to my body. As I turned, I took one look back to see if there was some kind of an answer. Nothing had changed and it continued to float nonchalantly around the room as if it was waiting for me to join it. I returned to the office and my heart was heavy with despair. I didn't understand why no answer came. Just a simple word or two telling me what to do from a messenger angel is all I had hoped for and needed. As I approached my body that still lie on the floor sleeping peacefully, I felt like I had failed in my effort to uncover my purpose in life.

I remember slowly sliding inside my dense, heavy body with a great sense of relief to return to something familiar. When I woke up a few seconds later, the room was pitch black and the entire experience was wiped from my memory. I looked up at the clock and only fifteen minutes had gone by since I had lain down to take my nap. I tuned off the heater, slowly stood up and walked into the front lobby. In a fog of amnesia, I unlocked the front doors and hurried up to my next job.

A few hours later I finished cleaning the exercise room and crawled up to my bed on the rafters. Minutes after I closed my eyes the music started and it began to lull me to sleep. I was completely oblivious to what had taken place a couple of hours before. At that time I did not know this was just the beginning of a series of events that would change the course of my life forever.

Chapter 3
SECOND OUT OF BODY EXPERIENCE

⌒☾

When I woke up that evening, my body felt heavy and my heart felt sad but I didn't know why. I slowly changed my clothes and put my shirt on inside out and backwards. My head spun and I saw black spots before my eyes when I carefully crawled down from my perch in the rafters. Dazed and confused, I slowly walked down to the pizza parlor to order a calazone for breakfast to clear my head. I loved this thick, folded piece of bread filled with cheese, tomato sauce, pepperoni, peppers and onions. Since I was really hungry, I ate two of them to give me the energy I needed to work all night.

Around ten that night, I left the pizza parlor and walked past the movie theatre, down the long corridor and around the corner to the spa. I placed my key in the lock, opened those two heavy wooden doors and the usual smell of sweat and chlorine greeted my nostrils. Wearily, I walked over to my storage closet and pulled out the spray bottle, squeegee and heavy vacuum cleaner to begin the nightly routine. My equilibrium was off and it took a great deal of focus and coordination to clean the mirrors and navigate the head of the vacuum around each Nautilus machine.

When I finished, I headed to the locker rooms and like a robot scrubbed the sinks, shower stalls, mats, and toilets until they sparkled.

I let out a sigh of relief when I entered the inner sanctum and saw the statues of the Greek gods staring out into the pool room. They seemed to have a source of knowledge that couldn't be shared because they were stone, yet it emanated from their faces. While I vacuumed the pool and scrubbed the Jacuzzi, I prayed and begged for an angel of light to come to me and tell me what to do. Tears poured down my face and my heart ached with grief. I was all alone and begged for a secret meeting between a messenger and me. No answer came.

When I finished cleaning the entire pool room at four in the morning, I turned off all the lights and headed to the office for my early morning nap. As I lay down on the shaggy carpet my back cramped up with searing pain from working hard for so long. In my mind I instructed my internal clock to wake me up in one hour. The carpet was damp from the foggy, ocean air so I turned on the little room heater beside me as usual. The warm air blowing from the fan helped the muscles of my back to relax and slowly lulled me to sleep.

I was stunned when I woke up less than a second later standing beside my body. I stared at my physical body sleeping on the floor and the realization hit me that this had happened the previous morning. A shock wave went through me as I looked at my standing translucent body. I bent down to touch my sleeping body but my hand sunk inside of it. I pulled it out quickly hoping I did not wake myself up. I thought to myself, "If my body isn't dead then I must be unconscious or in a coma."

Out of the corner of my eye I noticed that the lights were on in the Nautilus room so I turned and bolted through the open door of the office. Suddenly, I realized I was not walking; I was gliding and fear rippled through my body. I lost my balance so I lifted my arms to grab hold of something in an effort to steady myself. That is when I became aware that I had an invisible gyroscope inside to help me stay upright and negotiate my way around. It took a little while for me to acclimate to this internal navigation system and when I did, I began to relax and have fun, like an excited toddler walking for the first time. The exhilaration inside my body was uncontainable and I was able to move without restriction. I felt free like superman and now I could fly.

Instead of being stopped by physical objects, I could glide right through them. I moved with speed through the Nautilus machines and tried to navigate my luminous body around the corner. Instead of going around it, my translucent body went through the sheet rock and wooden studs of the wall and emerged out the other side. Then I slid right through the racks of dumb bells and stopped right in front of the panel of light switches. I put my right arm up to shut off the lights and it went right into the wall, behind the panel and came out under the light switches. Again my translucent body shuddered with the fear of being electrocuted.

Then I looked up at the ceiling at the numerous panels of florescent lights and noticed they were not on. Slowly it dawned on me that this had happened the night before and this light that moved around the Nautilus room came from a different source than the florescent lights in the ceiling.

So I focused my attention on the lights floating around the room and noticed they were much brighter than the previous night. This time the golden white light filled the entire room and an array of brilliant pinks, greens, blues and purples swirled throughout reminding me of the northern lights. They flowed gently around the room inviting me to join them.

Like a moth attracted to the light, my translucent body moved into them and I felt the energy in these lights pick me up and carry me slowly around the room. The lights wrapped themselves around my body like a warm blanket and permeated my luminous body while lifting and carrying me like a gentle merry-go-round. They radiated a soft love which sunk through my luminous skin. This felt wonderful until it started to sink inside my body to dissolve my pain.

But I couldn't let that happen. How could I trust this light when I didn't know its source of or its intent? I had asked it for months to give me my purpose but it had not answered me. How could I let go of my pain and open to it when it didn't give me an answer? For all I knew it was just trying to lull me into a blissful hypnotic spell of peace and love without giving me the answer to my question. I was terrified to let down my guard and allow this light to heal me.

It slowly dawned on me that I had a huge, thick scab covering my chest protecting my heart. The longer I drifted in the light the more it tried to dissolve it. In defiance, I crossed my arms over my chest and I told this light that I needed an answer to my question before I could let my shield down and allow it to dissolve the scab or heal the pain in my heart. In truth, this pain and hurt was all I had to hold on to and sad to say, it was part of my identity.

So I simply repeated my question, "What is the purpose of my life?"

I did not trust it and I needed to be told what to do by a benevolent being, not for it to try and heal me.

I continued to drift slowly around the room and I felt the quiet, peaceful energy in these lights. The beautiful aurora borealis colors floated around my body lifting me up and down like gentle, tropical waves on a sunny beach in paradise. As I floated around the room I noticed the lights reflected in the mirrors and then I saw my translucent body. I was made out of filaments of light that looked identical to my physical body which gave it a luminous appearance. I smiled when I noticed my arms were crossed in a determined sort of way across my chest.

After what seemed to be hours and no answer had come, I began to negotiate by saying, "Tell me what my purpose is and I will let go of my scab."

It was almost as if I knew what it wanted so I tried to barter with it saying, "Send an angel who will tell me my purpose in plain English then I will do what I am instructed to do."

That didn't work so I tried, "Give me a sign."

But no answer came in response to my negotiation tactics so I started to get angry and what I said then does not necessitate repeating. When I finished screaming at this loving light, I separated myself off in a huff and floated into the office.

I stood a few feet away from my physical body sleeping peacefully beside the heater debating whether to go back inside. I turned and looked back into the Nautilus room at these beautiful loving lights and realized they were not about to give me the information I needed. Then I looked back at my body and realized what a miserable existence I lived. I was a poor janitor making two hundred dollars a week working seven days a week, living in the rafters with nothing to my name with no reason to exist. I had to make a decision whether to stay in my luminous body or go back inside my physical body.

Then my responsible mind took over and rationalized that I had to finish my work. There was a whole other building to clean and the owners of the spa needed me to have it done by morning. So I reluctantly decided to return.

My luminous body cringed as it began to slide inside the top of my physical head. I became aware how warm, free and alive my luminous body was compared to how heavy and dense my physical body felt. Inch by inch I moved slowly into this cold, hard jello mold which encased me like cement. My head was the last to return.

Seconds later, I opened my physical eyes and gasped for air. My chest felt like it had a cement block sitting on it which made it difficult to inhale but easy to exhale. Breathing was extremely difficult and I had to focus on inhaling and expanding my lungs over and over until my breathing returned to normal. Blinking my eyes was very hard to do because my eyelids felt heavy like thick, black rubber.

My luminous body had not synchronized with my physical body and this was similar to the feeling I've had when my legs or arms had fallen asleep. I could not move my body as it seemed to be made out of a thick, heavy rubber. I tried to raise my arms but my luminous arms lifted right out of them. Then I tried to lift my legs and my luminous legs popped right out of them. I thought if I sat up my physical body would follow but when I did, my luminous body went vertical while my physical body remained on the floor. This was hilarious to me and I laughed but it posed a problem. I couldn't do my job if my bodies didn't merge and work together. Now that I had decided to come back into my body I couldn't retain my connection.

So I lie back down and set my intention to sink each luminous photon inside each physical molecule to merge them together. I had to create an energetic glue to get them to synchronize together so I focused my attention on one area at a time. I started with my luminous arms first to synchronize them up with my physical arms. Slowly the two melded and I could lift them up together but they seemed to have a loose connection. Next I focused on my legs. Each photon in my luminous legs became heavier as they merged with the cells of my physical legs. After they bonded, I lifted my legs a few inches off the ground and dropped them back down. They felt numb and tingly.

Then I focused on reconnecting the rest of my body so I could sit up. I was able to coordinate my luminous body with my entire physical body well enough to regain some strength to flop around on the floor like a fish that had just been pulled out of a pond and dropped on dry land. When I was able to gain control of my body's movements, I reached for the chair and pulled myself into a sitting position. Next I slowly stood upright and looked around the room. I was stunned to see the lights were gone and the Nautilus room was completely black.

When I took a few steps my legs wobbled like rubber and I nearly fell over when I bent down to shut off the heater. I slowly lifted my body into an upright position and staggered out of the office into the Nautilus room to see that no lights floated through it and it was quiet. I carefully turned around to look up at the clock on the wall and what seemed like hours had been only fifteen minutes. In a daze I slowly walked down the hallway towards the door and looked at my reflection in the mirror to see my luminous body was gone. Only my unstable human body was in the reflection.

If anybody had watched me walk out of those huge wooden doors that morning they would have thought I was very intoxicated. My physical body's coordination was completely out of balance and my legs were unsteady. I stumbled and staggered down the walkway like I was a puppet on a string. I could only focus on the ground and carefully placed one foot in front of the other. As I walked past the pizza parlor I bumped into the wall and nearly fell down. I managed to make it across the courtyard and over to the steps leading to the upper level. My hand grabbed onto the cold metal railing to pull myself up each step until I made it up to the top.

It was a long, painful walk that day to the exercise room and I found it difficult to get in the door to finish my work. My body was not cooperating with my mind. I was very confused and tears poured down my cheeks while I struggled to pull the vacuum out and clean the floors.

Questions tormented me, "Why had I felt so much love and not received an answer? Why was this light persecuting me? What would have happened if I had uncrossed my arms and let the light heal my pain? Why was I so stubborn?"

I finished cleaning and wearily crawled up onto the rafters and lay down on top of my sleeping bag completely exhausted, but sleep did not come that day. I was plagued by unanswered questions as I tossed and turned over the events of the last two mornings. I could not hold back my tears and luckily the music drowned out the gut wrenching sobs that poured from my heart. I was completely confused and my body felt like shredded wheat. When the music stopped in between classes, I had to cover my mouth to hold back the sounds of my body's uncontrollable weeping.

I kept telling myself to ignore what had happened the last two mornings and chalk it up to a bad nightmare. But my heart over ruled my mind. It felt real. It was as if the light had tried to gently lift off the scab to expose my wounded heart and a lifetime of anguish. I did not know that so much pain, anger, sadness and confusion could exist deep within me.

At the same time, I was humbled that so much love in that light could embrace me in my stubbornness. But I was also ashamed that I did not trust it. I had been temporarily freed from my body like a genie escaping from her bottle. I was liberated, unrestricted, unconstrained, unlimited and boundless. Then I chose to go back into my body in a fit of stupid rage to be a prisoner again. With these thoughts, I clenched my fists and pounded my chest in deep despair while the music blasted below and the instructors yelled to motivate their students clad in sweaty tights to keep in temp till the bitter end.

Night returned too soon and I heard the last aerobics teacher bid farewell to her students, turn off the music and lock the door. I crawled out of bed and made my way down the rickety wooden ladder. Indescribable pain and fatigue racked my body from lack of sleep. My only hope was to get a big meal and work hard all night to exhaust myself. Then I knew sleep would come.

Chapter 4
THIRD OUT OF BODY EXPERIENCE

༄

After eating a large sandwich from the deli, I slowly walked down the path to the spa and my mind continued to question what had happened, "Why had I been fully engulfed, lifted up and carried by this golden white light? Why had these soft aurora borealis lights caressed me to the point where I felt they were trying to tear the scab off? What was the purpose?"

When I thought about the scab, I looked down and felt it across the entire front of my chest. Even though it was only an emotional wound, I could feel it physically as if somebody had dragged me on the asphalt face down which bloodied the entire front of my body. When the blood had dried up, it created a thick layer of protection which held in years of blood and puss, that contained all the painful memories of my life.

My mind went round and round, like a hamster running on a wheel and my emotions went up and down like they were riding a roller coaster. I had asked this loving, soft light a simple question and all I needed was a straight answer. It didn't respond. Instead it just bathed me in its nurturing light that asked me in a silent way to let go of my hurt. On the second night it had grown bigger, brighter and stronger. It carried me around the room and I felt completely engulfed, caressed and loved by this light. My mind tormented me with questions, "How could something love me so much and be so powerful, yet not give me an answer to my purpose? Why did I feel that it knew the answer? Was it all a game designed to drive me insane? Was it just toying with me?"

I descended down the steps to the lower level and I walked past the pizza parlor, the movie theatre and down the long corridor to the entrance of the spa. My heart was not with me as I unlocked the big, wooden doors because I did not want to be there. My body felt like lead as I went through the act of cleaning the spa. It took every ounce of strength I had to spray the mirrors and drag the squeegee over their surfaces. My arms hurt with searing pain as I hauled the heavy vacuum cleaner around the room and pushed the beater bar back and forth, back and forth, extracting the dirt and creating those perfect parallel lines in the shag carpet.

When that was done, I wearily staggered ten feet behind my physical body into the men's and women's locker rooms and went through the motions of cleaning the showers, sinks, toilets, mats and floors in each room.

I finally got into the pool room where the statues stood waiting and my legs gave out. I collapsed to the floor weeping until nothing else would come out of me. My emotional body was completely empty. Even though my body and emotions felt dead my mind continued to ask, "Why did I even ask for my purpose? Why did I feel this way? Why I don't I just drop it and accept my lot in life of being a simple janitor? Why did I experience this loving light? Why didn't it talk to me? Why didn't it answer my questions? Why did it convey a feeling of love that wanted to permeate me?"

My rational mind just would not stop and it coaxed me to stand up and continue until I completed what I had started. I finally finished cleaning the entire place, shut off all the lights, walked into the office and laid down on the floor. I was totally exhausted. It was around four in the morning and I had been awake almost thirty-six hours. Even the purring heater couldn't lull me into unconsciousness. I tried telling my mind to shut up and my tense body just to relax and sleep because I needed it, but that didn't work.

I just laid there on the floor with my eyes wide open. Then I blinked. In that instant I was standing next to my physical body. My eyes were shut and my body finally slept. As I stood beside it the realization hit me that I had left my body in a blink of an eye and my luminescent body had slid out of the top of my head in a split second. It was easy, effortless and a total relief.

I bent down to shake my body to see if I could wake myself up but my hands went right through my left arm and into my chest. I quickly lifted my hands out and thought to myself, "Great, you are finally asleep and you can get some rest."

I felt sorry for my exhausted carcass lying on the floor and I told it I was finished being human and I was never going to return.

As my body rested in peace, I turned and floated into the Nautilus room toward the light and smiled. I knew it well by now and I was happy to see it this time. The light was drifting around the room and it was brighter than the night before. It filled the entire room with a magnificent golden white light which was filled with soft flowing pink, green, blue and purple lights creating a serene and peaceful environment to drift away into oblivion.

But something was different. I noticed a column of white light with sparkling silver particles pouring straight down from the ceiling right through the floor in the middle of the room. It seemed to be the answer that I was looking for so I glided quickly right into the center of this fascinating column of light and stood there. The silver particles that flowed through it carried an essence of a higher frequency and it made this light much brighter, yet it was still very soft on the eyes.

I stretched out my arms and noticed this circular light that flowed straight down from the heavens was about twenty feet across. I looked up and smiled as the tingling silver particles touched my face and soaked through my skin like a sweet summer rain. I put my palms up and laughed with delight as these silver particles tickled them and poured down into my luminescent body. This was invigorating and I knew it was trying to convey something to me.

I watched it pouring down through the ceiling and wondered, "Where is this coming from?"

Two ideas came to me right away, "Maybe it's a portal to another dimension and maybe it knows what I am meant to do with my life."

These thoughts sparked my frustration and I glared up at the ceiling, stomped my translucent foot with explosive anger and roared, "I will not budge from this spot until you tell me my purpose. I am not going to finish cleaning nor am I ever going to go back into my body to live a miserable existence. I will let my physical body stay there and they can hall it off to the hospital to decompose. You have to tell me my purpose right now. I will stand here until you tell me who I really am and what I came here to do. I have asked for months and I have been very patient. Now it is time for you to give me an answer."

I stood resilient in the eye of this silent storm. My strong stubborn nature held even stronger in my luminous body and I was determined to stay there until I got what I needed. After a while, I nervously shifted from one foot to the other and crossed and uncrossed my arms to prevent cramping in my legs and mid-back from standing so long. But it never happened because pain and fatigue did not exist in my luminous body; it was just a memory from my physical body. I put my hands on my hips and glared at the light pouring down from the ceiling. I was not about to give up and it seemed that it was not going to give out.

In amusement, I watched those bright aurora borealis colors gently swirl around me while the column of light with silver sparkles poured down through me like a gentle, loving waterfall.

But they were not going to dissolve my resolve because we had come to a complete and total stand off. I was self righteously determined to continue doing what I was doing and stubbornly refused to budge until I had gotten what I had asked for even if it took forever!

Chapter 5

ASCENSION

୧୭

The show down continued. I was totally defiant and the silver particles streamed faster down through my luminescent body trying to tickle me into submission.

The longer I stood there the brighter and stronger the aurora borealis lights became. Their colors increased in intensity and created a hurricane with no wind in anticipation of something unknown to me. The tempest grew and my mind reflected on what I had experienced. For two nights I had walked in the loving light and now I stood in a portal of light with silver particles that seemed to be a doorway to the answer to my question. I felt these beautiful silver sparkles tingle as they flowed down through my translucent body. I knew they came from somewhere and I was determined to go there. But I didn't know how I was going to do that.

Then my mind started to doubt my tenacious position. Would it be better to give up and work a job that had no meaning? Was it better to stay a self made slave? Was I destined to be a thankless janitor and live a simple meager existence rather than seeking my true destiny?

But something inside me kept persisting. I kept thinking there has to be more. I am not the type of person that just works a job to make money to buy things. My life has to have more meaning than that.

With this point of view, I looked back into the office to see my body laying there sleeping. I thought to myself, "Poor girl, she is so tired, tormented, hurt, with so many years of pain amassed in her body. She was old in her youth and aging very fast with no hope to her life."

After what seemed like hours of deliberation, I took a deep breath in, dropped my stanch determination and decided to give up for good.

Yet, in one last desperate attempt to receive an answer, I lifted my head and looked up into this light pouring down through the ceiling and begged, "Please tell me what I have come into this life to do?"

I stood there and waited a few minutes more. That was all, just a few minutes more and then that would be it. I would never ask again.

When no answer came, I slowly turned to walk back to my body and hung my head in resignation for the very last time. I looked down at my hands and stopped in shock. I was startled to see that they were beginning to swell. My hands kept getting bigger and bigger. Not only were my hands swelling but my arms began to expand. I was growing with the energy of this light and a tingling sensation moved from my hands, up my arms and into my body. Pretty soon my entire body had expanded to four feet wide and grown ten feet tall. Even though my luminescent body was immense it still had the same features as my physical body.

Then something wonderful happened. A powerful force within the intelligence of this silvery, white light began to lift me up very slowly. Instead of moving straight up I began to spiral in the fashion of the DNA helix. I was ascending. It was exhilarating and wonderful to move upward into this light. To where? I didn't know. But I was happy to say goodbye to my body lying on the floor in this world.

As I drew closer to the ceiling I wondered, Will I hit the ceiling and bounce back or will I disintegrate into nothing?" Regardless of my questions, I gently spiraled into the ceiling and up through the carpeting on the floor of the bookstore above the spa. I thought to myself, "This is great. Now that I am invisible and I can come into this bookstore to read any book I want at any time for free."

Instead of stopping to read a book, I continued slowly up through the ceiling of the bookstore and kept going up through the rafters and out the top of the building. Once above the roof, I stopped and hovered free from the restriction of my physical body, my grueling job and my miserable existence. I spread out my arms, looked up at the stars and laughed.

I happily floated above the building in this dark Monterey morning and looked west across town towards the beach while reflecting on the many sandcastles I had built while watching the whales migrate south. My body slowly turned towards the north and my eyes followed the bike trail that snaked into the little town of Seaside. I reminisced on the smell of the dried leaves that fell from the tall eucalyptus trees and crushed under my bicycle tires when I rode this path in the summer. I continued to rotate towards the east and scanned the evergreen pine trees on the tall hills surrounding the shopping complex. In the middle of these hills was my favorite park where I sat under my special tree on a lush blanket of pine needles to eat liverwurst sandwiches while I watched the children and dogs play.

When I came full circle, I spun around a couple of times to feel how easy it was to move in the air without getting dizzy. My luminous body was carried in an invisible force field of energy and I had finally acclimated to this freedom. I felt giddy with joy and I was so happy that I could have exploded with ecstasy.

Chapter 6
FLYING THROUGH THE GALAXIES

ᕲᕣ

This was completely different than being in my physical body. I was in seventh heaven and my arms and legs were stretched out as if I was going to make an air angel. An invisible force field held, supported and sustained any movement I decided to make. My heart was ecstatic and I could go as far as I wanted in any direction and never stop because I knew I was invincible. Fatigue did not exist here and my strength was available on demand. The sky was not the limit anymore because I was in a zone of power and I knew I could fly to the edge of the Universe and back again with no exhaustion.

I loved being liberated and when I looked down at my body, I saw a gigantic luminescent version of me. My out-stretched arms were the same shape as my physical arms but approximately one and a half feet wide. My legs were about two feet in width and both arms and legs were made out of strands of a see through bluish-white light. I was limber and flexible like a rubber band and I could have tied myself in a knot and untied myself in seconds. My entire body was sealed with a white corona that hummed with a powerful vibration. Even though my body was enormous, I was lighter than a feather.

As I slowly became accustom to the size, shape and energy in my newly discovered light body, I began to wonder why I was free from the gravitational pull of the earth and what would happen next. This new sense of liberation made me giddy as I floated in the dark night air and I thought about flying to an exotic location on this earth. That idea made the vibration of my luminous body begin to escalate and I knew I had to go somewhere. I could not just stay here and hover.

As I pondered on my predicament, I heard a voice to my right say, "Spin your spheres."

I was shocked. The voice sounded like a male version of my voice with a megaphone and it conveyed a powerful, commanding presence of authority. I quickly looked to my right expecting to see a person hovering there with me. I saw nothing but the black night sky.

Suddenly I felt a warm, liquid energy pour into the top of my head and down into my chest filling my entire body. This radiant fluid contained a force of knowledge that opened my interdimensional perceptions. I could hear everything and feel the atoms of the entire Universe. Next a wave of energy expanded my awareness and opened my interdimensional vision. The veil of illusion receded from my eyes and the limitations of the three dimensional world no longer existed.

Not only could I see forever in every direction but I gradually became aware of an enormous sphere around me which was approximately a hundred feet in diameter and over three hundred feet in circumference. The external wall of this sphere was about ten feet thick and it appeared to be a silvery-blue, translucent color. The interior was filled with shimmering white, silver-blue plasma that created a powerful force field around me.

I watched two more spheres materialize within the first sphere and I knew with my intuitive intelligence that these were the spheres the voice told me to spin. Their walls were the same thickness and their spheres were the same size and dimensions as the first sphere and they rested comfortably superimposed within it.

I also understood from the liquid transmission I received that I was to use the intent in my breath to activate their rotation. I paused for a moment and laughed because my human lungs couldn't even blow up a balloon and now I had the internal wind power of the Greek God Aeolus, son of Poseidon. The spheres waited silently while I pondered the inevitable.

Then I focused and with gusto filled my luminous lungs, set my intent to initiate rotation and exhaled to spin the spheres. With fascination I watched as my breath set up a ripple in the plasma and spread out in all directions. This wave of intention poured into the walls of the spheres and they began to spin, one to the left and the other to the right. The movement of the walls began to set in motion the inner particles and they spun in circles flowing through each other setting up a counter rotating plasma field. I was surprised that they did not collide with each other. Instead the walls moved right through each other and they became a unified force field that activated the inner particles creating bluish-white plasma. This began to build up a charge inside the sphere which affected my luminous body with a powerful vibration.

I was delighted to hear these spheres spinning in rhythm with my heartbeat. This helped me understand the true power of their relationship with my life pulse. I knew these spheres were connected to my human body's heart and they were responsible for the activation of my heart beat before my birth as well as the source of it during my life.

The force field of the spheres kept building and getting stronger and stronger preparing for interstellar space travel. Then they slowly began to lift me up and quickly propelled me towards the stars. I automatically looked towards the Pleiades and a memory flashed in my mind of being a young girl lying on the lawn on a hot summer night. My little finger pointed to the Pleiades and in a confident voice I said, "I am from there."

Now I was returning to visit my previous home. The spheres revolved faster and the force field got even stronger as they lifted me up towards that magical star system that was my place of origin. In a blink of an eye I was flying around the Pleiades. I had spinning spheres that gave me the ability to go to any star system I chose and I could only imagine what I looked like as I blazed around each star. I could not stop and visit because I was on a mission to find my destiny. Pretty soon I was spinning circles around the entire Pleadian system and building up greater speed to dash out towards another galaxy.

Now I was finally free to fly from one galaxy to another instantly and there was no limit to where I could go or what I could discover.

Chapter 7
OUT OF THIS UNIVERSE AND INTO CREATION

෨

I left the Pleiades and zipped on to the next galaxy and the next one. There appeared to be no end to the constellations, nebulas and other indescribable star systems. To see them close up was amazing and to describe them would take words that I don't have. Each planetary composition that I explored took me further out and deeper into the cosmos.

As I jettisoned from one star system to another, there was nothing that could stop me except a question that entered my mind that brought me to a stand still in mid flight, "Why haven't I been given my purpose?"

My mind kept going with its query, "Here I am tripping through this universe and I still don't know what my destiny is? Why?"

I would have thought by now I would knew everything but all I had acquired was the knowledge of how to spin my spheres and soar though vast, uncharted territories.

While I hovered there watching and listening to the spheres spinning in rhythm to my heartbeat, I heard the voice beside me speak again, "Spin your spheres faster."

Again, I quickly looked to my right to see if someone was floating by my side, but no one was there. A warm, liquid light poured into the top of my head, down through my body and out into my spheres. It transferred and activated a vast multi-dimensional knowledge and a deeper intelligence within me as well as the spheres. I watched this liquid energy flow out and realized these spheres and their wisdom had always been with me. I had just forgotten about them because I couldn't see them with my physical eyes.

I complied with the voice's instruction and I took a big deep breath in, on the out breath I spun the spheres faster. The walls of these spheres began to hum with a tremendous but silent vibration as their rotation speed increased to the rate of a baby's heartbeat. The first sphere held and fortified the force field of the spheres as their power increased exponentially.

As the spinning spheres powered up, I watched all the spheres merge into one. They became a unified field and turned into one translucent sphere filled with a luminescent, bluish, silver energy. The intelligence within this force field did not deem it necessary to adventure through the rest of this universe; instead it propelled me right up to the outer limits of all the star systems.

When I reached the edge, there appeared to be a white embryonic membrane that held the universe together in an expanding and contracting translucent envelop. Even though I could feel it holding me in, I found it easy to slip through as my sphere created an opening which allowed me to pass. The membrane closed behind me and I moved into a vast, silent, dark pool. It was pitch black and void of everything yet it contained an energy vibration that was more powerful than the deep space that held all the stars, galaxies, solar systems, nebulas and constellations that I had just flown through.

I looked all around and I saw other universes equally spaced through out this black void. They looked like giant monoliths filled with smaller orbs of light. Each universe looked the same as the one I had just left and they orbited slowly around each other in suspended animation throughout the black void.

I zoomed by all these universes passing them one by one until I came to the end of the field of universes. The intelligence within the sphere carried me out further into the darkness and I came up against a thick, black, dense wall that reminded me of tar. It was as if it wanted to hold me back and not let me go any further. My sphere created a portal and carried me right through it. It was then that I realized this wall was a barrier that held everything inside the void in a pool of limited dimensions. Everything was subjected to the illusion of form, limitations, time, beginnings and endings. Once I was on the other side I felt myself expanding in many ways, not just in my energy body but in my intuitive awareness.

As I moved further out into this black space I came to another wall which seemed to be thicker. It tried to hold me back even more than the first one but my sphere used its innate wisdom to open a pathway. Its resistance seemed to dissipate and the wall particles separated to let me transition through it. As I moved out into deeper space, I expanded even more spiritually, structurally and dimensionally which increased my knowledge exponentially.

Then I came to a third wall and this one was very, very thick and it seemed impossible to get through it. My sphere simply created a gateway and propelled me through to the other side. As I emerged, it was as if I had come all the way through to the end of the black void and stopped.

I gasped as my luminous body with its humming sphere slowly moved into a magnificent light which was brighter than the sun at high noon on a white sandy beach in a tropical paradise. The love in this light gently caressed my body like cotton candy and welcomed me home. I moved deeper within it to experience more of it. My hands reached out and it softy accepted me with the tender touch of its delicate golden, white light. It slowly permeated my hands and moved up my arms and into my body. I took a big, deep breath and its light filtered into the scab covering my chest. I finally let down my guard and trusted this light to melt it away. When the scab dissipated, the deep pain and hurt began to spill out of me dispersing into the light. My luminous body convulsed with exquisite pleasure as the waves of liquid grief and sorrow left me and melted away into nothing. It dissolved and merged completely into the light.

I floated deeper into this loving light and it continued to saturate my being with its nurturing and loving peace. I felt safe and content to allow it to become me and I to become it.

My luminous body began to dissolve and I was just one being returning home bringing my cellular data bank of information like a drop of water falling from the clouds into the vast ocean. I realized the infinite intelligence within the particles of Creation was now downloading all of my experiences into its vast, endless library. Every memory I had of every incarnation spread out returning to eternity and filling the knowledge photons with everything that I had created in every incarnation.

I watched the sphere dissolve as it entered into this endless light and a powerful insight rose up inside of me. I remembered forming the sphere when I left Creation and now it was returning to the source of its origin just like me. Not only had it been with me from one incarnation to another, but it held the memory of my entire journey. Now that I had reached my destination, I didn't need it any more so I let it go. As it dissipated into the light, its entire memory and all of its experiences returned home.

I saw and I understood that when everything in all of the universes and the black void return home, they will bring with them the ultimate memory of all that was created and can be created to rejoin the eternal light. Each atom within the cradle of illusion contains the memory of the past, present and future and will return to the light of infinity to prepare for the next master piece of Creation.

Then my awareness expanded out in all directions and I understood everything was accessible at all times. I had finally crossed over the threshold from not knowing to all knowing. I did not need to store it anywhere or retrieve it from a data base because it was in me.

I moved further into this benevolent light and I could see it went on for infinity in all directions. I no longer had limited vision and I could see forever. I knew I was matter merging and becoming antimatter. I still held onto a few memory particles of my luminous body while I was slowly integrating light particles into me. I was expanding out and I knew at one point I could explode and become infinity. I would be the vast ocean of light and become all the experiences that had ever happened and would ever happen. I was uniting with Creation and finally returning home.

Chapter 8

THE VOICE OF CREATION

ᙡ

Suddenly, a benevolent and powerful voice interrupted my journey into bliss by saying, "This is what you call God. This is Creation and there is no end to it."

I did not look for a deity this time because the voice came from all around me and I knew it expressed itself from this light. I also knew that this was the same voice that had guided me here and it was stronger here because it was in its element. This voice did not come from a consolidated form but from the infinite intelligence within the force of eternity. It was the Voice of Creation.

A thought emerged from within me, "That sounds right. I like this much better than what I was taught."

A memory momentarily drifted into my being and I reflected on my childhood years in the Grace Lutheran Church where I heard how God was a jealous, angry, and judgmental masculine being. Then I realized that I had come to earth to be filled with these thoughts, belief systems and limitations we collectively created.

I knew differently at that moment so I let the memory dissipate and become the source of all knowledge. Nothing could stop me now because I had let all these fear based beliefs disperse. Now I saw everything differently as my body continued to move deeper and deeper into Creation. Small particles of my form separated and dispersed into the light like salt dissolving into water and with it went my identity and my connection to my body. I could completely let go of it and it would be okay. I no longer had to maintain my personality or self. I was going home and did not have to hold any thought or form because I was now becoming infinity. Each part of my limited, third dimensional composition that dissolved into nothing was replaced with particles of joy, happiness, wisdom and a soft loving light. I was in ecstasy, bliss and a state of euphoric rapture. I was home again in the power of Creation and this was where I truly came from. I couldn't wait to completely dissolve into nothing because I knew I would expand out to become everything. I was becoming Creation again, so I set my course to remember everything and disappear into the light.

I moved further and further into this expanding light and the Voice of Creation interrupted my progress with a direct order and said, "Turn around."

I replied, "No, I am not going back and I am not going to look back and turn into a pillar of salt."

In my defense my dissipating luminous mind was referencing the Bible story of Sodom and Gomorra. In the story Sarah was leaving the city as it was being destroyed and when she looked back, she was instantly turned into a pillar of salt which ended her life. Not me. I was not going back nor was I going to look back at that hell hole that I lived in.

Then I realized it was just a story I had experienced on earth and I could let that go as well. And I did. It slowly dissipated out of my reality and returned to the beginning and end of everything.

In defiance I kept going, moving deeper and deeper into the soft, loving light. The excitement of becoming this infinite intelligence propelled me even faster. My being absorbed into its benevolent power and the pleasure of becoming the master of Creation again pulsed through me and drew me even deeper. I was delighted to become a magnificent being.

The Voice of Creation interrupted my rapture into the light and said in a commanding tone, "Turn around and look!"

What was left of my luminous body was brought to a standstill. Just by the tone of its voice I knew I could go no further. I knew in order to continue merging with Creation I had to do its bidding.

I slowly turned around and looked back at the void that I had just come through. I saw all the universes suspended in the black energy field within the void that kept them orbiting around each other. My vision was completely different than seeing with my physical eyes. I could see everything because my perception had been opened completely and it was as if I was the creator observing Creation. I was completely open and saw into all dimensions and there was no limitation to what I observed. As I looked deeper, I noticed that all the universes seemed identical with their individual galaxies, solar systems, planets, nebulas, and many indescribable formations. I could see my universe and inside of it was my earth where my body lying asleep on the floor imprisoned in my three dimensional world and I said, "I am not going back there."

The Voice of Creation ignored me and stated, "You as the creator created all of this!"

I stared at my physical body on earth and said, "That's impossible. There I am lying on the floor trying to live in a three dimensional world, scraping by every month and eking out a meager existence. I work eight hours a day, seven days a week and I created all of this?"

I couldn't comprehend how that could be possible so I crossed my luminous arms in a defensive posture and asked, "How did that happen?

In response the intelligence within the Voice of Creation opened up a vast memory window. It looked like a massive, cosmic, IMAX movie screen playing out the first film ever made.

First, I saw this beautiful ocean of light that went on for infinity and never ended or began. It was an eternal light. Then I watched as the light rolled itself back from its very center creating a vast, round, black pool. Lining its edges were three, thick black walls that acted as dimensional barriers giving anything that entered or exited this black pool the true experience of resistance and dimensionality. This pool was completely void of everything yet it had the same power, love, intelligence and wisdom as the light. It was designed to hold the masterpiece of Creation.

The Voice of Creation explained what was happening by saying, "You as Creation pulled back the center of the light and created the void which is also known as the cradle of illusion. Then you as the intelligence within the force of Creation began spiraling the light away from Creation and down into the void to bring about the cosmos. With your divine intelligence and magnificent wisdom you created planets, galaxies, nebulas, and constellations of all kinds. These star systems you grouped together and spun them into formation thus creating many massive universes. After they were formed, you moved them into place and synchronized them into orbit around each other which became the field of universes."

I watched this take place with jaw dropping awe. The memory continued to play out as the Voice of Creation resumed, "Once the void was filled with all the universes, you as the creator decided to separate from Creation and individuate to experience everything within the void. With your infinite intelligence, you spiraled yourself away from Creation and formed your light into massive comets. You brought with you the wisdom and power to create and this became your first experience of division and separation."

The silence was deafening as I watched the light spiral itself away from its source dividing into massive comets of light. These comets of light poured out of Creation and down into the void. I could feel the pain of the first separation and I screamed, "No, don't leave, don't go down there!"

But they continued. Then I noticed each comet had a long tail of light streaming behind it which remained connected to Creation. Even though they were undergoing the experience of separation, they were still connected. Nothing could stop them; they were ecstatic like children running and screaming out of the classroom to play. They streamed from all sides of Creation into the void towards the universes.

As these massive comets encircled the field of universes within the void, they paused in unison. The intelligence within them decided to experience all the universes simultaneously and they exploded into as many comets as there were universes. When they separated, I noticed their tails divided as well to keep their connection to Creation while they continued to experience the illusion of separation. The force of Creation was strong within them as each comet sped towards its chosen Universe. They were elated and knew exactly where they were going.

When the comets entered into their perspective universe they stopped again to prepare for the next phase of their adventure. With a deep, innate wisdom each comet exploded again and became as many comets as there were solar systems, galaxies, nebulas and constellations. They streamed down inside and entered into their chosen star systems with their tails still connected to Creation.

I watched all of these comets pour into all the star systems within each universe searching for the form or shape of existence they were to become. These omnipotent comets of light disappeared into unidentifiable energy masses while others took on unfamiliar and indescribable forms.

The Voice of Creation interrupted my focus by saying, "Some of you decided to go to Earth which is the deepest, darkest, densest dimension you can go to experience everything that you are not and everything that is opposite of you. You also went there to have total amnesia of your true identity."

Shock waves rippled through my luminous body as I watched comets of light stream towards earth and pour into human bodies. This information shook me to the core of my being.

The Voice of Creation did not pause but stated, "You asked for your purpose."

My body reeled again with the shock of being reminded that I was the one who had begged and pleaded for months to receive this information.

It repeated, "You asked for your purpose. You asked to know what you came to do in that human body on earth. I will tell you what it is. Your purpose is to go back and bring people to their soul and to Creation. By doing so you will help them remember who they really are, where they came from, what they always have been and what their true purpose is in their chosen lifetime. Once you have reconnected them to the love, light, wisdom and power of Creation, then they may return as emissaries fully conscious of their soul's destiny."

Chapter 9
DISCLOSURE OF MY DESTINY

ℭᴠ

The Voice of Creation had spoken the unthinkable. I was shocked, stunned, flabbergasted and floored. I had finally received my answer. What I had asked to know for months had now been given to me. What I had been so tormented about was released in those simple words, "Your purpose is to bring people to their soul and to Creation."

It was so simple, so easy and true now that I was standing in this infinite ocean of light totally filled with the power of Creation. It was wonderful to receive my divine purpose and I knew it was my fate in life and my divine destiny.

But, I also knew that it was an impossible mission to fulfill. From my perception Creation did not understand what it was like to be human nor did it understand what it was like to be in that three dimensional world. That is when I decided to try to explain what it was like from my perspective.

I pointed towards my earth and emphatically stated, "You do not understand. People do not care about their divine purpose. All they care about is their jobs, cars, money, status and things. In fact they don't even care about each other and they don't care about their soul and their connection to Creation because they don't remember. And I would be a stupid idiot to go back to earth and try to do this because nobody wants to know their true destiny."

I continued to hammer the point home saying, "Then you have the government, military, millionaires and corporations who have all the money because their lives are based on total greed and mind control. They are malicious and they use, abuse and hate the minions. They are selfish, inconsiderate, and inhumane and they treat each other like trash. They do horrible things to each other such as kill each other and derive pleasure out of it."

I was now yelling at the top of my lungs and I was not about to stop. "Further more, when they have screwed everybody out of everything and amassed fortunes, then they live miserable lives, terrified that someone is going to take all their money, power and processions away from them."

When I finished giving Creation a piece of my mind, I turned away from my earth and the Universes, bolted and flew into the light. I was never going to live in my human corpse again on that three dimensional earth to be picked apart by vultures. I had changed my mind and I could care less about fulfilling my divine destiny. No one was going to stop me from returning home this time, not even the Voice of Creation.

My body began to dissolve again like ice melting in the warmth of the sun. In total defiance I put my luminous arms up into the air and screamed, "I am not going to go back to fulfill my destiny and you can not make me!"

All that was left of the years of pain inside of me poured out and dispersed in the soft, benevolent light. I was becoming less of this luminous form and merging with what I had always been. I was now totally free and returning to infinity.

Chapter 10
RELUCTANT RETURN TO EARTH

ᕬᕙ

As I moved at warp speed into the light, I felt a pair of luminous arms wrap around me and embrace me with an unconditional love so strong it brought me to a complete stop. Slowly these arms began to pull me backwards. Everything was in reverse and my dissolving body of light began to take form and shape again. The structure of my luminous arms and hands grew back and solidified. I was being dragged kicking and screaming through Creation against my will. I did not want to go back for it would destroy me to return to my body and know that this infinite light filled with its sweet unconditional love was here. I would never be the same again.

As I was carried to the edge of Creation and into the void my sphere returned. My heart began to sink with a deep sense of loss and there was no use fighting anymore because these arms of light were in control. We moved rapidly through the thick walls of the delineations of dimensions which tried to delay our progress but failed. These walls restricted and compressed the atoms in my body and I became heavier and denser.

The light of Creation slowly disappeared behind the walls and I felt lost as we moved backwards through the void and into the field of universes. As we slipped by each one I looked inside and saw the magnificent star systems within them.

These arms of light wrapped around me even tighter when we entered the embryonic wall of the universe I had just left and my heart filled with an even deeper sadness. We descended down through all the constellations, nebulas and galaxies I had seen before. Then we rapidly dropped into the galaxy that held the solar system that I was to return to. We did not slow down but kept moving with great speed towards my earth and rapidly entered into its atmosphere, continuing in the direction of my city and down through the roof of the building I knew so well. We made our final descent through the ceiling and down into the room where my body lay. These loving arms of light tried to slide my luminous body right inside of my physical body but I refused to let that happen. Instead, I hovered about an inch above my physical body which was still sleeping peacefully on the damp, shag carpet. Without any parting words the arms of light unwrapped themselves from around me and ascended through the ceiling abandoning me there to survive on my own.

I fought the thread like filaments and the auric ectoplasm that rose up from my sleeping life form to engulf my luminous body welcoming me back. My fight continued as I wrestled with this magnetic force field for what seemed the better part of an hour trying to make my way back up through the ceiling and out to Creation. Then I had this simple thought, "I had better finish my work."

In response my luminous body relaxed and I knew it was time to return to work. Then I began to argue with myself, "Why did I even think that? What is wrong with me? A few minutes ago I was in Creation not wanting to come back and now I am ready to be a slave again?"

With those notions I gave up the fight and sunk strait down into my body. A split second later I opened my physical eyes and gasped for air. I couldn't move. My luminous body felt mummified inside my physical body. It was a very strange feeling like being trapped inside of a cold, dead corpse. When I tried to move, my luminous body would not lift any part of my physical body because it seemed to be made out of a heavy, thick black rubber. Instead my luminous arm would just lift right out and every time this happened my body would ripple with laughter. I tried to sit up and my luminous body would bolt upright while my physical body lay perfectly still on the floor.

I realized I had to use my intention to synchronize my luminous body inside my physical body to get them to merge like the previous night, so I focused on one area at a time. First I started with my arms. When I went to lift up my physical arms, my luminous arms came right out of them, so I had to repeat the process of sinking my luminous arms into my physical arms until they bonded. When the atoms of light sealed with the physical molecules, I lifted my arms a few inches from the floor and they quickly flopped back down. They lacked strength and felt numb like they had pinched nerves. The skin began to tingle and the blood began to flow into them again. I laughed out loud because I felt so helpless.

After I got my arms moving I concentrated on my legs and I tried to lift them but the same thing happened as with my arms. So I focused my intent to submerge my luminous legs inside my physical legs until they bonded and I was able to lift my physical legs. I looked like a fish out of water flopping around on the floor trying to regain my coordination. Then I tried to stand up but my legs were very wobbly so I grabbed hold of a chair to steady myself.

The chair appeared to be full of tiny, spiraling sparkles that moved within the confines of its shape. These energy sparkles shimmered brighter in the aluminum arms of the chair and slower in the black padding of the seat. I thought I was just dizzy and they were just the black spots I've seen when I was about to faint so I blinked my eyes quite a few times to wash away the distortion in my vision. Not only did it persist but I noticed the wooden desk had these spinning particles in it. Slowly it dawned on me that I was now seeing the energy field of all physical objects. It was quite fascinating and I could have stood there all day and watched the moving particles but I had work to do.

I looked at the clock and to my amazement only one hour had gone by. The spa was dark and quiet. There were no aurora borealis lights floating around the Nautilus room nor was there a column of light with silver particles streaming down in the center. I was back in my body and it was time to leave. Slowly I approached the big mahogany doors and my hand awkwardly inserted the key in the lock, turned it and I pushed the door open using my shoulder. It took a huge effort to relock those doors and make my way slowly past the theatre, pizza parlor and up the stairs. My body was heavy and I walked like a zombie past the retail stores and up to the aerobics center.

I slowly unlocked the front door and went to work but it was different now. I became aware of a warm light in my heart which contained the knowledge of my purpose as well as the conscious reactivation of my soul's connection to Creation. I was a new person and I knew where my true home was.

As I pulled out the vacuum, I noticed it was alive with the energy spirals similar to the ones I had seen in the chair. I flipped the switch to see the tiny sparkles jumping faster and that made me laugh. How could I take my job seriously when everything was alive? Even the squeegee and spray bottle had moving energy molecules in them.

When I looked into the mirror I saw dazzling colors flow in and around my physical body and moved where my body moved. If I moved foreward quickly the colors would stretch like elastic behind me and they took a while to catch up with my body. Seeing this made me giggle and that changed the entire color of my field making it a greenish-orange. I stopped to stare at it and it turned a bright yellow. Then I spun quickly in a circle and the colors swirled around me like rainbow sherbet.

This made me very hungry and the thought of eating ice cream brought a memory to my mind of a special time in my life as a little girl when I helped my daddy change the sprinklers in the orange and avocado orchards in sunny California. Once we finished our work, we headed for the local Thrifty's Ice Cream shop for a scoop of rainbow sherbet in a sugar cone as my reward. That memory made me cry. I slowly wiped the tears from my eyes to see a reflection in the mirror of a gray mass forming around my heart and pouring out of my chest. When I stopped crying the mass dissipated into thin air and the bright colors returned making my body a happy playground. I was clearly becoming an emotional basket case.

It was difficult resuming my cleaning career because I felt like a kid in Disneyland where all the solid objects came alive as if they were popping popcorn and Mexican jumping beans while my mind tried to hold everything together in the way it was before. What took me minutes previously now seemed to take hours and my mind had developed an extreme attention deficit disorder. As I vacuumed the foot prints out of the carpet my mind raced at the idea of fulfilling my purpose while the colors distracted me from my work. It was the slowest I had ever performed my job.

I finally finished and put everything back in its place in the closet just minutes before the first instructor was to arrive. Then I crawled up that rickety ladder, carefully slipped into my sleeping bag and dreamed of my future.

Chapter 11
DAWN OF MY MISSION

༄

I awoke with a huge jolt late that evening from the buzzing of my alarm clock calling me to work. I felt like I had been somewhere in my dream time working on the matrix of my future and returned too fast. The little hand on the clock pointed to ten and the realization hit me that I was late. But, I didn't care any more because my life's purpose had changed. I was on a mission from Creation and I had to find a way to reconnect people to their soul and take them home. Once they re-established that link consciously, I had to bring them back into their three dimensional bodies as the force of Creation.

Even though my mind had no idea how I was going to accomplish my assignment that soft glowing light within my heart gave me the loving confidence I needed to figure it out. It also conveyed to me that I needed to look beyond my self imposed prison called my job and research my options in this three dimensional world.

As I crawled out of bed and climbed down the ladder, my hands gripped the sides which were made out of solid pine but they appeared to be filled with crawling black ants. I screamed, let go of the ladder and fell to the ground. At first I thought there were ants all over the wood but when I focused, I could see the wood was transparent and alive with tiny, black and white atoms that spun in circles like miniscule yin-yang symbols.

It was then that I realized my perception of reality had changed. During my visit to Creation all my senses had been completely opened and they stayed open after I returned which gave me the ability to perceive all dimensions simultaneously.

I grabbed hold of the ladder again thinking I could stop the atoms from spinning but it didn't faze them one bit. Then a soft voice from my heart said, "This is what the energy force looks like in everything."

I let go of the ladder, stood up and looked around. The walls and the carpeting were moving with these tiny atoms.

My stomach growled and I realized I was faced with the daunting task of leaving my sanctuary and finding food. So I headed out the door and up to the grocery store to buy breakfast. Shopping was quite an event because everything in the store was alive with movement and color. A simple decision to buy cheese, bread and juice turned into an adventure in the twilight zone. The plastic wrap on the cheddar cheese was a florescent orange and the cheese was filled with sparkling white lights like radioactive mold. The whole grain bread had spiraling brown molecules in it that reminded me of tiny worms squirming in the loaf. The juice was cold to the touch and alive with glowing lights which reminded me of sea plankton.

While I picked out my dinner, I noticed that people's bodies were alive with these spinning molecules. They also had beautiful colors rippling inside and outside their bodies while sending out temporary energy cords to each other as if to connect for a moment. Then the cords dissipated as they went on their way. I had to keep telling myself to not stare because I could not take them aside and tell them what I saw. They would think that I had just gotten out of the loony bin.

So I kept my mouth shut and quietly observed the phenomenon of the shopper's energy fields while I purchased my groceries. Then I headed for the nearest picnic bench and sat down to make my sandwiches. I examined each slice of bread to make sure it was not infested with worms and I carefully sliced the cheese looking for mold. As I placed the cheese in between the slices of dry bread and took my first bite, washing it down with the juice, I had to tell myself to relax because I was not eating worms, radioactive mold or drinking plankton laden sea water. What blew my mind was that everything looked and tasted the same as it had before but now it was alive with energy inside my mouth.

A moment later tears began to pour down my cheeks as I took another bite. I was going through the biggest shock of my life with nothing to stabilize my reality. But sitting out in nature that evening and watching the squirrels jump up on my table to beg for food gave me a sense of comfort. I could talk with them and they would understand. I told them about the spiraling atoms in the food, picnic table, bushes, trees and everything around me. After I finished talking they stared at me with those hungry eyes as if to say, "Stop your worrying and give me something to eat right now."

I dropped pieces of my sandwich on the ground and they gathered round chattering with delight while clutching the bread and cheese in their precious little front claws. Then they ran off and disappeared into the forest.

My stomach was full and I realized it was time to go. It was after eleven that night when I opened those heavy, wooden doors and walked into the spa. My physical eyes could see the normal world as well as the moving atoms of energy in it. It was a very different way of perceiving reality because I was seeing with eyes deep within my head that looked through my physical eyes and I knew they were my soul's eyes.

I touched the Nautilus machines, bar bells, metal chairs and wooden desks. My hands grasped their physical form which was rock solid and motionless but my eyes saw that they were filled with millions of tiny spinning atoms. They were held together by the intelligence within their shapes and it didn't matter if it was wood, metal, glass, plastic, stone or cement. My whole world was now alive with energy.

When I finally started cleaning it took all my focus to complete each task and I worked straight through till early morning. Then I headed out the door and up the stairs. When I came to the top of the stairs, I heard strange music with voices that was not the typical piped in mall music. As I strolled towards my destination, I realized that what I was hearing was not just one type of music or words; there were many and all at the same time. I was listening to twenty radio stations simultaneously. I thought it would stop when I unlocked the door and walked into the aerobics room but it didn't. I tried to make heads or tails of the music and conversations but most of them were garbled and in different languages. My head was acting like a multi-channel receiver and it was as if I had the radio stations from the entire world playing inside my head. I could listen to all of them simultaneously or focus on one at a time.

I had a pretty strong and level head on my shoulders and it didn't bother me one bit that I was seeing and hearing all of this. I spent a little time in nature every evening which helped me cope. I just thought to myself that it would wear off and soon my perception would return to normal. But it didn't, in fact it got even stronger.

After a few weeks I decided to go to the library and research paranormal experiences. I read many near death stories and learned they had experienced a deeper opening into multidimensional perceptions and a deep rejection upon returning from the light. I had just opened the doors to altered states and I was seeing and hearing with my expanded sense perception all the time.

Now that I had read that others had experienced what I was going through, I could settle into my routine with all my doors of perception open and enjoy it. All I did was work, eat and go round and round in my mind about what I was supposed to do and how I could do it. I had no idea how to go about fulfilling my purpose.

Then one day a bright idea emerged from my heart, "If I go to school maybe the teachers would know what the soul is and how to access it because they inspire so many students."

At the age of twenty three, I called the local high school and asked how to get my diploma. They said that class was in the afternoon and I could start anytime. Since I worked all night, I figured I could sleep until two in the afternoon, then go to school, eat dinner and go to work.

Shortly after making that decision, I found myself sitting in a classroom full of students of all ages. Most of them wore dark Goth outfits with dyed black hair and rings or studs through their noses, eye brows, lips, tongues, belly buttons and rows of them lining the edges of their ears. I was in the problem kids' class. After my first week I realized these kids were trying to hold onto their uniqueness. They rebelled against rules and regulations that did not allow them to express their individuality and creativity. Instead of getting their desired recognition, they received negative attention. They were free spirits expressing themselves in a world that could not take the time to understand them. I could see the lights in these kids' eyes when they talked about what they loved and how they expressed their soul's essence.

I finally got up the courage to ask my high school teacher, "What is the soul?"

She answered, "I don't know. Look it up in the dictionary."

This shocked me because I thought that teachers were trained how to understand kids. But in reality they were taught to teach out dated material and control the class neglecting the inner soul of the student.

The day of my graduation finally arrived. The ceremony was a small one but it was it was very important to me. The principal handed me a glowing piece of parchment sitting inside a red leather binder stating that I had completed all the units I needed to finish high school. It gave me a wonderful feeling of accomplishment but it didn't give me the information I needed to take people to their soul.

Since I had not found anyone who knew what the soul was, I decided to continue my education and search even further to find out how to fulfill my purpose by going to college. I applied for grants and received what I needed to go full time. I felt that one of these teachers would know for sure what the soul was and how to connect with it. I asked my astronomy teacher what the soul was and he replied, "We know that there is something in us but we don't know what it is."

The most profound experience I had was working on the cadaver named Fred in my anatomy class. He was stored in a special room and kept in a black bag. I walked in that room the first day, slowly unzipped his bag and stared. I noticed his eyes were wide open and asked, "Are you in there?"

My teacher, Butcher Banes, laughed and told me I could lift up his chest which had been previously cut open and touch his heart to make sure he was dead. Instead of facing my fear that he might come back alive when I looked inside, I zipped up the bag and worked on memorizing various body parts lying on the tables. Everyday at the end of class I would unzip Fred's bag and check to see if he had come back to life. At the end of the first week I finally mustered up enough courage to touch his heart. It was cold, hard and not beating. Wrapped around his heart were gray lungs filled with bits of black charcoal from smoking cigarettes. I was hooked. Even though his soul was gone and he smelled like formaldehyde, I was determined to examine and memorize every part of his body, four semesters in a row.

Attending college full time and working all night finally took its toll on me and I sadly resigned my job at the spa. It was a bittersweet goodbye because it had held many experiences that had helped me grow in so many ways. It had been my home and a special place of awakening. Now it was time to move on.

Chapter 12
MY SOUL'S PURPOSE FULFILLED

❧

College turned out to be a blessing in disguise. One serendipitous day while walking down the hallway to my class, I saw a flyer on the school bulletin board announcing a psychic fair in the school cafeteria that weekend. The contents of the flyer sparked my interest so I went. It turned out to be a mecca where people spoke a different language of the spirit, its purpose and the deeper meanings of life. Readers sat at tiny tables and read cards, palms and divined the future. I was so excited to be there that I signed up for many readings.

The information I received that day opened up a whole new world that spoke to my heart. When I sat down at the first table an older woman with white hair piled on the top of her head taught me how to write a letter to God asking for what I needed. Immediately after that, I went to the next table and there sat a middle aged lady with brown hair who took my birth date and read my future using numerology. The next reader had me gulp down a cup of tea and then she read the pile of tea leaves on the bottom of my cup. Late that afternoon a thin, young man drew a picture of my aura and told me what it meant. At the end of the day I sat down with a gypsy woman who told me my future in detail reading the regular playing cards and my palms. She was very old and sick but managed to cough her way through the session.

I was so impressed with the information that I decided to follow in all of their footsteps and learn to do readings. Once I made that decision, I met a dear life long friend that invited me to help her with smaller psychic fairs that were held monthly at the Boy Scout Hall in Carmel, California. At each fair I would spend time with individual readers learning divination using astrology, numerology, palmistry, tarot and discovering the secrets hidden in the regular playing cards.

The knowledge that I attained was quite extensive yet my search for the soul continued so I decided to go to massage school. The training was intensive and the hours were long but I slowly became aware of a warm glowing light around every client that I touched. When they first lay on the table it was not that apparent. After an hour or two of nurturing massage the light around their bodies began to expand. Sometimes bright colors would flash on their skin and other times pastel blues, greens, oranges, pinks and purples would cascade around their bodies. I knew I was touching the energy field of their soul. Months later, when I received my certification of completion, I had already built up a full time practice with a regular clientele; but it wasn't enough.

My heart longed to fulfill my destiny and my focus turned to healing, so I decided to attend Barbara Brennan's School of Healing which was located outside of New York City. This required that I take five, one week long trips a year from Monterrey, California to Ronkonkoma, Long Island.

It was here that I learned how to understand and work with the spinning atoms and colors that flowed through and around people's bodies. Now I was able to use my gifts of perception to watch the healing energy from Creation flow into my heart and out my hands. This opened up a powerful vortex for the psychic surgeons from the fifth dimension to work through me. When I held this fifth dimensional portal open my mind went silent and my body temperature increased till I broke out in a sweat. Then my body began to vibrate while gentle streams of light poured into the top of my head, down my arms, out my hands and into my client's bodies. This set up an energy field that allowed the psychic surgeons from the fifth dimension to heal their blocks, wounds or illnesses. Attending this healing school was the best decision I had made so far and it helped me advance one step closer to my goal.

It was during this time that I saw my first soul and it did not happen in the way that I expected it to. One evening around Christmas time, a tall silhouette of light in the shape of a human stood in front of me hovering for a long time.

I inquired, "Who are you?"

No answer came; this being just floated in the air waiting for something. Then I asked, "Why are you here?"

It replied, "I have come to teach."

I expressed my thanks for it sharing its intent and told it to leave. I was shocked to see it begin to condense and spiral its form into a ball of light the size of a baseball and head straight for my belly. When it penetrated my abdomen area it felt like something gently punched me. I doubled up and cried out in amazement because it felt like a phantom pain. A few weeks later I was pregnant.

During the nine months that followed, I became aware of an orb of heat that would enter and exit my body through the top of my head. When the heat poured down through my body and into my belly, my baby would start kicking. After a while my baby would stop moving and this orb of heat would rise up through my body and out the top of my head. When I watched it ascend into the sky, it seemed to follow a beam of light and disappear into the heavens. Many photos were taken of me with an old camera during my pregnancy and they captured a spiraling light above me or a large spherical light around me.

After my baby boy was born he continued to enter and exit his little body through the fontanel on the top of his head as an orb of light. Every month I took one picture of him and put it in a photo album. Around the age of three he had grown into a blond haired, blue eyed angel and loved to paint at his little easel. I snapped a Polaroid picture of him with his paint brush in hand and slipped the developed picture inside the photo album with the other pictures. Then I slowly turned the pages back to the first pictures when I was pregnant. I stared at the white orbs of light a long time and he ran over to see what I was looking at. His little hands grabbed the book and he pulled it towards him looking closely at the pictures.

I pointed at the orb of light in one of the pictures and asked, "What's this?"

He looked at me in disbelief and yelled, "Me!"

I laughed and asked him, "What did that orb of light come here to do?"

He jumped up and down with excitement, then he dashed around the room and said, "I came here to teach, sing, dance and play ball."

His mind had retained his soul's purpose and I was so grateful that he had let me take pictures of it. He continued to talk about it with his little words and I thought to myself, "Out of the mouths of babes comes the wisdom of Creation."

A year went by with a move from Monterey, California to Sedona, Arizona which was known as the spiritual capital of the world and it brought about a significant change in my career. I was a mother, massage therapist, healer and now I was asked to practice my medical intuitive gifts at the Red Rock Spa which was owned by a very special lady.

Clients would come and go but there was one extraordinary day that I began to take people to their soul. A woman walked in and booked a medical intuitive/aura reading. I looked at her field and asked out of the blue, "Would you like to go to your soul?"

She replied immediately, "Yes!"

My body shook in response with fear, excitement and curiosity. My mind tortured me saying, "What in the world do you think you are doing? How are you going to do that?"

It didn't matter because I could see her soul and it was enormous. I told my mind that my heart knew what to do and it was time to trust its wisdom. One hour later she was in tears and fully connected to her soul and its destiny. I went home that day and collapsed in shock and disbelief. I had finally begun my true purpose in life and it had only taken fifteen years of research, training, experimentation and spontaneous curiosity.

The next week the owner of the spa introduced me to a burly man who stood about seven feet tall and clutched a Bible in his hands. He told me that he had just been released from prison after a seven years sentence. During his incarceration he would pick up the Bible and his hands would shake, then his body would heat up. He asked me if I could help him and I said, "Sure!"

Throughout that session his body shook with a powerful vibration and sweat poured down his face. The room became a sauna and he connected to his soul which took him to Creation. He accessed his purpose and told me his destiny was to return to prison as a volunteer and help the men free their souls. He left that day no longer traumatized from his past and walking on air.

Over the years many more people came to transform their lives by reconnecting to their Soul and going to Creation.

Chapter 13
CONCEPTION OF THE SOUL

❧

Cheryl walked into my office, plopped herself down in the pink chair and started to cry. She was a petite lady with brown hair and hazel eyes. Alligator tears poured down her cheeks as she reached inside her purse, pulled out a small zip lock plastic bag and handed it to me saying. "Please tell me what's wrong with my baby?"

Stunned, I gently took the bag, held it in my hands and carefully examined what appeared to be a tiny, solid, white mass surrounded by a red liquid. Still sobbing she continued, "This is the third time I have miscarried and no one can tell me what is wrong. I don't understand. I gave birth to my son three years ago and the pregnancy was normal."

She reached into her bag, pulled out a picture of her son and handed it to me. He stood proud like Hercules with his muscular arms wrapped around the necks of two full grown huskies. The glint in his dark eyes and the smile on his face showed his imaginary power and dominion over these lovable fury creatures.

In one hand I held a picture of the fruit of her womb and in the other a baggy containing her unborn child. I told her I was not qualified to diagnose the contents of the bag and she would have consult with her medical doctor.

As I spoke I couldn't help but notice with my soul's eyes the silhouette of a child standing behind her as if waiting for another opportunity to be conceived. I explained to her that the soul of her miscarried fetus was close by her and asked her if she would like to meet this child.

She wiped the tears from her eyes and asked, "How can we do that?"

I invited her to lie down on the massage table and focus on her desire to have this baby. She lay down, folded her hands on her solar plexus area and began to relax. At the same time she focused deep within her heart and located the feelings she had for this child. I instructed her to rest inside the middle of her heart and sense the presence of the child.

A few minutes later she said, "I feel like something is standing by the right side of my head."

I told her to take her time and focus carefully, sensing with her high sense perception to perceive if it felt like a girl or a boy.

Three minutes later she stated emphatically, "It's a girl."

Next, I instructed her to let those feelings lead her imagination and visualize what this girl looked like.

Instantly she replied, "She is so beautiful and tiny for her age. She stands about two feet tall, long curly brown hair, dark penetrating eyes with long eye lashes."

I prompted her for more information, "How old does she appear to be?"

She responded softly, "Three."

Then I asked her, "What is her name?"

Cheryl began to laugh, "She said Sam, short for Samantha." Then she moaned, "I really don't like the name Sam, but the funny thing is I was going to call her Samantha. It didn't dawn on me that she would use the nickname."

Now it was time for the mother to find out all about this little girl whose soul stayed through three miscarriages. Mother and daughter conversed like old friends getting to know each other.

While they talked the unborn daughter told her that she needed to come into a body to have her words heard. In the spiritual dimension no one could hear her speak. Her mother was amazed to hear her strong voice and feel her determination to be born.

I began to ponder how I would get these two connected so Cheryl could conceive her. Then an intuitive insight came to me. If I could get Samantha to show her mother her soul then maybe the child would bond with the mother.

So I inquired, "What does her soul looks like?"

Cheryl focused on her child for a while and stated, "She is showing me a light which is big and bright like the sun."

I was curious how this enormous sun would connect to her mother so I asked, "How can Samantha bond with you and be conceived?"

To my surprise Cheryl replied, "She wants me to stop eating pepperoni pizza because it makes my body weak."

Both of us laughed. This was not what we had expected but it answered the question Cheryl presented earlier about the cause of the miscarriages.

When we finished laughing I asked Cheryl again, "How does Samantha wish to be conceived?"

Suddenly, Cheryl gasped and tears began to pour out the sides of her eyes. She took a big deep breath in and said, "Samantha just condensed her soul into a tiny ball of light, brought it in the top of my head and sank it down into my heart. It feels like a ball of fire."

Her back arched as she described this ball of energy filling up her chest with heat. Then she explained in detail how she felt this light sink down towards her belly and into her uterus.

I watched this compressed ball of light navigated its way slowly down the left fallopian tube and sink itself into the holographic heart of the egg within the left ovary. The egg began to glow and a soft light rippled out expanding all around the mother creating a pulsing aura of light. What amazed me was the innate spiritual intelligence inside this tiny ball of light that guided it to its resting place.

When Cheryl left that day a smile had replaced her tears. She went home ecstatic and one month later called to inform me she was pregnant. Eight months later Samantha was born at home weighing six pounds and measuring nineteen inches in length. She was very healthy and had a very strong set of vocal cords for a new born.

Four years later Cheryl brought Samantha to visit me and this precious soul matched the description her mother had given in my office: Petite, black, curly hair, beautiful dark eyes and a boom box for a voice. As the years went by Samantha displayed incredible leadership abilities and to this day she is involved in school plays, year book clubs and public speaking groups. She is indeed expressing her soul as her mother watches her grow into a woman.

Chapter 14
ANIMAL COMMUNICATOR

☙

Betsy, a young successful veterinarian from Ohio, walked into my office after being diagnosed with the Epstein Bar Virus. She arrived with her husband and two children and the look of fear and desperation showed on all their faces. Because of her illness they had seen their world come apart and watched as their lives unraveled and descended into the depths of despair. Everyday the family prayed for a miracle but no solution came.

I took her hand and lead her back into my healing room to lie down on the massage table. Her voice was barely audible and labored as she continued to explain the hopelessness of her situation.

The virus had taken its toll on her thriving veterinarian practice and she could no longer work eight hour days or help her desperate clients with their sick animals. She woke up every day exhausted and relied on her family to do everything from the household chores to cooking her meals as well as helping with what was left of her practice. Her husband had taken over most of her responsibilities by running her office. If she did manage to walk out the front door of their home, down the sidewalk and across the driveway to the building next door which was her place of work, she could only work for two hours at the most. Then she would lay down to sleep on a cot set up in the back room.

Her petite body was thirty nine years old but she was very thin and looked almost fifty. Her sandy blond hair was thinning prematurely, her blue eyes were sunken and her skin was pallid. She looked like she was wasting away.

Slowly I switched my vision from my physical eyes to my soul's eyes. In her solar plexus area were small vortexes which allowed a small amount of yellow energy to pour into her body to support her thinking and speaking process. I noticed three cords emanating out of this area, one to her husband which was two inches in diameter and taking in a bright white light to nourish her body. The other cords flowed out to her children. They were smaller with a soft yellow light flowing out through them into their solar plexus areas giving them what little energy she had left.

My soul's eyes were drawn to the rest of her energy vortexes which seemed to be collapsing within themselves and could not take energy in to nourish her body. The auric layers of energy around her body felt stagnant and appeared to bathe her body in a gray color which did not allow its energy to nourish her body.

As I read her, I felt this overwhelming death wish inside of her and I told her that it felt like her body wanted to die. She broke down and sobbed telling me that was exactly how she felt but she was not ready to go. I recommended instead of fighting this feeling that she permit herself to be curious and follow it to its source. With my instruction she slowly sank into the depths of despair inside her body and tears poured down her cheeks as the thought of leaving her family surfaced. I encouraged her to stay with it to take her deeper into the very core of its inception.

Many memories surfaced into her consciousness that were linked to this but there was one that kept repeating itself. She described it as a fuzzy, warm feeling almost like being inside water. While she focused on this sensation, she saw a tiny embryo and realized it was her. I encouraged her to imagine holding it in the palms of her hands and asking this little one what she felt.

When she did this she heard, "Mommy doesn't want me."

In response her adult body started shaking with fear. I encouraged her to ask the little one where this knowing was located in her little body. In response the little one pointed to her heart and showed her a black mass. Then I asked her to focus on it to discover what it was. The little one began to convey to the adult that this was where she had taken in rejection from her mother and held it there because it was the only form of love she would ever get.

Slowly the little one descended into a very deep place of total despair and said, "I might as well give up and die."

This energy mass inside her heart had fully saturated every cell in her little body shutting it down.

Shock waves of horror rippled through her adult body as the realization hit her that this is why she felt like dying. The impact of this memory from her developing fetus overwhelmed her senses. It was very painful and too much to bear.

This awareness triggered other memories. She recounted being the ninth of ten children and her mother saying to her that she was just another mouth to feed, diaper to change and nothing special. At the time she understood what her mother had said and accepted it, but now the puzzle was slowly taking shape as she was putting the pieces together.

Other memories surfaced and she reflected on the first days of school. Her little body had taken her mother's fatigue and carried it off to kindergarten at tender age five because she had wanted to help her mother be bright and happy like she was. By taking rejection and fatigue away to another place this would create a vacuum for happiness to return to her mother. Once her mother's body filled up with joy then she could share that with the little one. But that never happened. Blame, shame and responsibility hid under the little girl's cheerful smile, bright eyes and hyperactive body while she played at school.

This is when I asked Betsy if she had this black mass of rejection inside her adult heart and she sadly said, "Yes."

After a few minutes she stated, "I have to heal this or I will die."

Then I instructed her to tell the little one this truth and ask her what the rejection needed. The unborn fetus responded immediately, "To be wanted, loved, needed and someone to listen to me."

I told Betsy to ask her what would symbolize those unmet needs. The little one smiled and showed her the colors of the rainbow. The adult instinctively poured all the colors of the rainbow around the little ones body telling her, "I love you. I am going to take care of you and give you everything you need from now on. You will be with me and I will show that I want you, I need you and I will listen to everything you have to say."

With this promise she slowly lifted the tiny embryo out of the womb and told her, "You are going to come with me now."

With my instruction Betsy asked the unborn one, "If we were to scoop out that black mass in your heart and replace it with what you really need, what would that be?"

The little one replied, "Trust of my light."

As she said this, the little one showed the adult this beautiful, soft light that was hidden below the black mass.

Betsy felt it and asked, "What is that?"

The little one replied, "This is the light of my soul. It has always been there waiting to be let out."

At my prompting they scooped out the black mass in her little heart and the adult's heart and replaced it with this sweet, gentle light. As they did this together the adult asked the little one to tell her all about her soul.

The little one described how her soul had come from Creation to help animals and talk to them. She showed her how to look into their eyes to feel how they felt. It was through those feelings that she came here to compassionately communicate with them with her heart, help them feel love and to recognize the soul in each one of them.

The little one continued to share her wisdom with the adult by telling Betsy that something was missing in her office protocol. She explained the animals saw her as an indifferent person wearing a white straight jacket and acting like a robot. They needed her to put down her clip board, listen with her open heart and speak from her soul.

The little one reminded her of Snooker, the little black and brown terrier with hives, who took in his owner's anger and just needed to tell her with his big black eyes that it hurt him. Remember how he would just stare at you as if to say something and when you tried all different kinds of medications none of them worked. If only he could have told you so you could have shared his feelings with his owner. Dogs have emotions, too.

She continued by helping her to recall Pepper the Dalmatian with the weeping eyes who was crying for her mother and needed more love from her owners. They never played with her or showed her any affection.

And then there was Tabby, the orange tom cat that never moved. He was just depressed and needed a kid to play with that would appreciate him instead of being cooped up alone in the apartment all day.

Memory after memory poured into the adult's awareness from the little one regarding the deeper source of these animals' illnesses. Betsy felt as though she had awakened from a deep coma and it all became clear to her why she had become a veterinarian.

With compassion Betsy whispered to her inner child, "Come inside my heart and from now on we will use this deeper form of communication from our soul with all the animals and their owners."

As Betsy placed the little one inside her heart and said, "From now on we will keep this connection to our soul and Creation strong within our hearts. I will check in daily to access our Soul's intuitive wisdom to use in my adult life"

As Betsy opened her eyes a beautiful spark came alive in them. She breathed deeply and all her energy centers slowly opened and her auric field began to glow. She smiled and said, "I feel alive again!"

When Betsy walked briskly out of the office her family gasp in unison and her children ran up to her and asked, "What happened?"

She smiled and told them, "My soul has been reactivated; it feels like my life force has returned."

Her husband smiled and they took hands and they walked together out the door into a warm, summer day to play with the children by the Oak Creek just down the hill from my office.

Three years later, Betsy came back for a visit and told me when she had returned home and walked into her waiting room, its cold, sterile environment begged to be changed immediately. Within a week eco friendly rugs covered the white tile floors. Dogs and cats roamed the office greeting the clients as they walked in the door. A big wicker basket of toys sat by the front door and two love birds softly cooed in their large cage in the back corner creating a fun, yet serene atmosphere. Plants and trees were placed in every room turning her place of work into a jungle. Her office had become a sanctuary and everyone loved it. Relationships with clients and their owners were strengthened with longer office visits and a deeper explanation of the pet's illnesses and their sources, followed with positive suggestions and treatments.

A year later, Betsy began teaching classes in animal communications where she told her students that all we have to do is open our hearts, listen and in time that small voice of intuition comes.

Since Betsy has resumed her career and it required many hours of caring for animals and teaching, she has learned over time to take care of herself with nutrients, loving her body and listening to her intuition. Today she is in perfect health.

Chapter 15
SOUL OF A MEDICAL DOCTOR

༄

B right yellow leaves had begun to fall from the Mulberry tree in my back
yard and the bulbs had just thrust their first shoots out of the ground
when I got a call for help from a doctor in Los Angeles by the name of Lester.
(Of course, you know this is not his real name but the story is true.)

When he called he spoke of intermittent heart fibrillations and a con-
stant burning pain in his solar plexus area that wouldn't go away. All his
scans showed he was fine and the doctors said he was healthy as a horse. But
the symptoms continued and he needed a medical intuitive reading. In our
conversation he said he had given up all hope of healing until a dear friend
told him about her visit with me and how I had helped her understand and
heal the deep pain from the fibromyalgia that incapacitated her body. He
said he would be passing through Sedona to visit his sister in a couple of
weeks and asked if I would be able to see him.

We booked the session and two weeks later he arrived at my front door
step looking tall, lean and quite healthy. As we walked into my office, he
spoke of his dedication to his career as a surgeon and the love he felt for his
wife and two kids. Then he slipped off his loafers, crawled under the soft,
pink blanket and looked me square in my eyes saying, "I am very scared
that I might die from this and I am not ready to push up the daisies yet."

I assured him that we would do all we could to get to the bottom of this
and heal it, but I encouraged him to trust himself and honor what feelings
came up for him in the session. Then I switched my vision from my physical eyes to my soul's eyes and scanned his energy field from head to toe with
my high sense perception. The energy center on the top of his head was
closed and area in his forehead appeared to be a gray brown color. His throat

had a silver band around it which looked like duct tape that hampered his ability to express his feelings.

What I saw next shocked me. A deep, red gash ran from his collar bone all the way down the center of his chest ending at his belly button. I was really excited and curious about the source of this anomaly, so I placed my hand above the energy gash and felt heat emanating from it. Pulses of energy from the heat flowed up into my hand and images of a little boy holding a knife flashed inside the screen of my soul's eyes.

I muttered something about a young boy holding a knife and to my surprise Lester broke out laughing. He laughed so hard it brought tears to his eyes. Then he told me at the age of four a neighbor girl named Tina had done open heart surgery on him with a butter knife while he lay naked on a wooden crate in his dad's garage. With her imagination, she had surgically cut open his chest and lifted out his beating heart. Then she handed the butter knife to him and said, "Now it is your turn to cut out my heart."

With no hesitation he took the knife in his little hand while she undressed and lay down on the wooden box. With confidence he placed the knife between collar bones and pretended to perform open heart surgery. He imagined cutting her chest open and reached inside. Just as he began to pull out her heart his mother walked in and screamed, "No!"

She continued to scream in horror as she grabbed the knife out of his hand and spanked him. Then she sent him to his room to stay in solitary confinement for the rest of the day. Tina was sent home and never allowed to play with him again. His mother never spoke to him about why she had such an intense reaction.

While Lester told this story, tears rolled down his cheeks and a great sadness filled his heart. I recommended that he honor his feelings and go into this sadness to visit this inner memory. So he did. In his adult imagination he went back in time and found his four year old inner child curled up in the closet in his bedroom crying.

The adult asked the little one, "Can I come in and sit with you?"

The little guy looked up in disbelief and said, "Yes, if you want."

The adult slowly crawled into the closet and put his arms around him and asked, "Can you tell me how you are feeling?"

The little guy responded sobbing, "My heart is gone and Mommy hurt me."

The adult inquired further, "Where do you feel that hurt in your little body?"

The little guy pointed to his bottom and then he pointed his finger towards his throat and brought it down the front of his body. The adult asked, "Can you show me what that hurt looks like?"

The little guy showed him a deep red gash that went all the way down the front of his body and then showed him an empty place inside his chest where his heart had been.

Tears came again to the adult's eyes as he told his little guy, "I know how you feel and I have that same feeling inside my big chest and I need your help in healing it."

The little guy's eyes lit up and he volunteered, "I just need my heart back and mommy to talk to me like she really cares for me and loves me."

In an effort to fulfill his little guy's needs the adult asked, "What can we use to represent loving and caring?"

To which the little guy replied, "A pink heart and a grassy green playground!"

Next the adult intuitively poured the white light of love and healing all around his little one cocooning him and said, "I love you. I care about you and I will give you everything you need. From now on you are going to be with me."

Little Lester began to feel as if he had a friend who understood him and he could trust to take care of him. That is when the healing and bonding of the adult and inner child began to take place.

After a while the little guy said he felt better, the adult picked him up and said, "Let's go have a talk with Mom and then we will get your heart back."

They went to have a long imaginary talk with their mother and spent time going over the details of that afternoon to understand why she had acted out of fear. During their conversation the adult realized the little one had taken in his mother's angry words into his little body and still held them in the red gash in his chest.

So he asked his little guy, "If we scooped out those red angry words and replaced them with what you need, what would we replace them with?"

The little guy smiled and said, "My pink heart so I can play."

Together the adult and the little guy scooped out all the angry words, the fear, and the red gash in both of their chests. Next they replaced it with a pink heart. Both of them turned to their mother and forgave her, thus releasing and letting go of all the deep seated patterns of anger and hurt.

Then they said goodbye to her and in their imagination they went over to Tina's house to ask her for his little heart. She was happy to see him and placed his heart back inside his chest where it belonged. Tina took little Lester's hand and led him out to the sandbox in her back yard to play. As they piled the sand high to build a sandcastle the little guy told her it felt nice to have his heart back because it was his connection to his soul. He said to her, "My pink heart knows I am an angel and I came here to help sick people."

The adult sat on the edge of the sandbox and listened. He knew exactly what his little guy was talking about because he had always dreamed of starting a recovery center for people who had been through surgery. It would be a safe place to delve deeper into the real cause of their illnesses to understand how it had formed in their bodies and to express what it needed in a safe environment. Then they would be able to heal the underlying causes and live without the fear of the illness returning to their bodies. He could teach them techniques to help them laugh, play, have fun, be happy and love themselves again.

While the two little ones played in the sandbox, the adult followed his vision into his future and saw himself fulfilling his dream.

In closing, Lester tucked his little guy into his heart and left my office that day walking on air.

Two years later I received a letter from him with pictures of his new center and some of the smiling people he had helped. At the end of the letter he said, "After I left your office that day the pain never returned and my heart has been ticking just fine. Your guidance inspired me to follow my true spiritual path and fulfill my destiny by helping others to heal their illnesses and fulfill their dreams. My heart will always be grateful to you."

Signed,

Lester

Chapter 16
SOUL HEALING FROM A PAST LIFE

❦

K en carried a large manila envelop into my office and pulled an x-ray out while telling me that he had renal failure. He pointed to his left kidney on the film, which appeared to be white similar to the bones of his spine in the picture and said it had stopped functioning about two years ago in the summer of two thousand and one. He had spent quite a bit of time with his doctor undergoing many tests to see what the problem was and how to fix it. His doctor ruled out all possible diseases saying he could leave it inside his body to atrophy or have it removed, either way it was not going to function again.

Then Ken turned to me and stated, "I know there is a solution and I hope you will help me find it."

I raised my eyebrows in response and told him that I would do my best to help him. With my hands, I gestured towards the massage table and instructed him to lie down and relax. I told him we would explore this together and see what came from the innate intelligence in his kidney.

After he lay down, I switched my vision to my soul's eyes while I sunk my energy hand inside to slowly scan and feel the kidney. My body started shaking with an indescribable fear and the longer I stayed inside the kidney the more intense it became. I told Ken that I was feeling a great deal of terror in this area which appeared as white and red strands of streaming light that flowed from his mid back area down his legs and out his feet. I kept hearing "Don't cut it off," over and over again.

I asked Ken, "Did you ever have something cut off of your body?"

When I said those words Ken opened his eyes wide and blurted out, "I was circumcised when I was six years old."

His face suddenly turned red and he tried to hold back the feelings that welled up inside of him but the tears surfaced and he began to weep. After that wave of emotion subsided he told me that memory had been buried for so long that he didn't even consider that it might be linked to his kidney.

I queried, "Would you like to go back into that memory and find out what you stored in your body from that experience?"

He wiped the tears from his face and said, "Yes."

Then he closed his eyes and I guided him back to the six year old and asked him to look into the little guys eyes to feel what he felt at that time. He had not been circumcised at birth and at the age of six the tip of his penis had gotten infected which quickly spread into his bladder and up inside his kidneys.

He finally got up the courage to tell his parents when the infection had gotten so bad that he almost passed out from the pain that radiated up his back every time he tried to urinate. They rushed him to the doctor where he was given a local anesthesia and his foreskin was quickly cut off. Even though the doctor had given him pain killers and antibiotics after the surgery, his entire pelvic and mid back area continued to experience searing pain for a couple of months.

It slowly dawned on him that this experience set up a trauma which imprinted a memory inside his little body that haunted his entire life with a deep fear of death.

I asked Ken to ask his little one if he felt like he was going to die. The little one responded with information that shocked him by saying, "Yes."

Then he pointed to a thin, wispy dark curtain to his left and said, "I was buried alive. Come, I need to show you."

He took the adult's hand and began to drag him through the veil and into an unearthly scene which appeared to be in England. It was night time and the fog was quite heavy as they ran down a cobblestone street towards an old white church. They came up to a wrought iron gate that stood between the disintegrating plastered side of the church and a tall crumbling stone wall. The boy pointed to the grave yard behind the wrought iron gate and said, "We are almost there."

His little hands pushed hard against the rusty gate and it screeched as the metal dragged on the stone walkway. They slowly made their way across the cemetery past rows of short head stones. He dragged the adult to a long pile of dirt and the little guy exclaimed, "Here it is!"

The adult asked, "What is it?"

In frustration the little guy yelled, "It's us. It's where we have been buried and we're not dead!"

He pointed to a little bell on the ground that swayed a bit making a barely audible sound. He dropped to his knees and started digging with his hands. The adult found an old shovel on a new grave mound and borrowed it to help unearth his past life. The ground was still soft and they quickly dug down to a wooden box and pried off the lid.

The little guy reached down, grabbed the hand that emerged from the box and pulled with all his strength. The adult joined in; together they lifted a young man from his premature coffin and brushed the dirt off his tweed jacket and trousers. A tweed cap fell from his pocket and he bent down to grab it, slapped the dirt off it and put it on his head.

His eyes sparkled and he smiled saying, "Thank you for saving my life."

The adult asked, "What happened? How did you get inside that coffin?"

He said he had come from Scotland to help his aunt when her entire family had come down with the plague. The day after all of them died he had climbed a tree in the back yard to cry. As he was climbing down he slipped and fell to the ground which knocked him unconscious. When locals came to get the bodies they thought he was almost dead so they threw him on top of the cart and carried him off to the cemetery. He woke up in a dark, cold pine box with a string tied to his hand and tugged on it for hours hoping someone would hear the bell. Days later he had died an unfortunate death which sealed his soul in that box and squelched his dreams of becoming a doctor.

The adult was shocked how vivid the past life memory played out and the impact of this young lad's words. Now that he had freed his soul's memory from the past it awakened his ability to remember his hopes and dreams in this life. He had always wanted to be a doctor but had become a pharmacist because the money was better.

I instructed him to ask this young lad if he wanted to go to the light or come with him into his adult life to fulfill his soul's destiny.

The young Scottish lad quickly replied, "I would like to come with you into your life and study hard to become a doctor."

The adult laughed realizing that he would have to go back to school and change his career, but he knew it was the right thing to do. So he took this young man's hands and invited him to come into his life and inspire him to fulfill his purpose.

At this juncture, I reminded Ken about his inner child that still held the trauma in his body from the infection. So I instructed him to focus on his inner child and ask, "What do you need?"

Little Ken replied, "I need to be safe and not be afraid of dying."

I was curious and asked, "What would little Ken like to use to symbolize that?"

After a few minutes little Ken whispered, "A sand box filled with all kinds of trucks, graders and back hoes with the sun shining on me to dissolve my fear."

With my guidance, they slowly scooped out the trauma and fear in both of their bodies and replaced it.

I wondered if little Ken wanted to become a doctor as well and inquired, "Do you feel your soul's purpose in this life is to become a doctor?"

The adult smiled and little Ken spoke through him about trick or treating on Halloween as a kid. He frequently wore a white jacket and stethoscope over a green shirt with matching pants. A green surgeon's cap sat on top his head keeping it warm. Little Ken's dream was sadly discarded just like his costume when he entered college and his parents let him know they expected him to take care of them when they retired. So he had to pursue a lucrative career in the pharmaceutical industry.

I brought Ken back to focus on his inner child's soul by asking him, "Where did your little guy hold that dream inside of him and what does it look like?"

Little Ken responded by pointing at his chest and showing the adult a pulsating golden star inside his precious heart.

Then I asked, "What is that star?"

Little Ken responded, "It's my soul and the star came here to help heal people."

I asked the adult Ken if he felt that star in his heart and he said, "Yes."

Then I asked him, "Would you like to become that star with your little one and see where it comes from?"

The adult laughed and together they merged their stars and journeyed back to the light they were before they came into this body. They spent quite a bit of time remembering the infinite light and vast love they had always been. They also remembered their soul's purpose to help others.

When it was time to return, the adult instructed the inner child and the young Scottish lad from the past life to jump inside his heart to create a bond of safety. He promised to love and protect them as well as take the steps necessary in his life to fulfill his destiny.

Ken slowly got off the table that day deep in reflection. He expressed his concerns about making a career change in his life at the age of forty and the impact it would have to his income.

I grabbed his right hand and showed him the life line in his palm and said, "You have a long life so take it one day at a time and listen to your heart. It knows what to do."

He smiled in agreement, got into his Ferrari and waved goodbye.

Ten years later a small white Honda drove up to my house late in the evening and Ken jumped out. He knocked loudly and when I opened the door he smiled and asked me if I recognized him. I did and invited him in. We sat on the couch and he told me when he left my office and returned home, he had quit his job and sold everything he owned to attend medical school. When he graduated he had enough money left to buy a small clinic in the town where his parents lived. He pulled pictures out of his pocket and showed me the modest clinic he owned as well as a nurse he met that became his wife. He was delighted to tell me that she was pregnant and their baby was due in three months.

He said, "Not only am I helping the sick to get well, I have many devoted employees and they have successful careers. I also take care of my parents since they retired last year and now I am going to have a family of my own which is a dream come true and that makes me very happy."

Then he looked into my eyes and asked, "Do you remember my kidney?"

I laughed and said, "Of course."

He whispered, "It's working just fine."

Chapter 17
GALACTIC INTERVENTION

෬

Nick came to see me in the early autumn, two thousand and four with a phantom pain which started in his left hand and traveled up his arm radiating into his chest. He told me that previous MRI's and Ultra Sounds showed no damage to his nerves, ligaments, tendons, muscles or heart. Every attempt to relieve his agony with high doses of pain killers and frequent cortisone shots failed to get rid of the problem but helped him continue working at various construction jobs. When the side effects of the drugs became too much to bare, he tried herbs, massage, acupuncture, reflexology and energy treatments but they didn't alleviate the searing pain in his arm or chest.

I looked him straight in his eyes and told him that it may be time to lie down and sit inside the pain to discover its source. He shrugged his muscular shoulders and said, "What do I have to lose."

Then he lay down on the table, closed his eyes and wrapped his right hand around his left wrist.

I instructed him to breathe deeply into the pain and set his intention to find its epicenter. With each breath he tried to sink deeper and deeper to find the midpoint. After five minutes he moaned, "There is nothing happening."

He continued to squirm with frustration and finally stated with disappointment, "I'm sorry but I can't find anything. There is just nothing there."

A few minutes before he reached this conclusion, I had switched my vision to my soul's eyes and scanned his body. I saw red beams of energy slither up through his nervous system, around the bones in his left arm and stream into his chest wrapping themselves around his lungs and pouring into his heart. Shielding this anomaly was a thick, white coating that looked like a plastic milk carton which enclosed the entire upper half of his body.

I was curious why he could not get through this stuck place so I asked him, "What is stopping you?"

He became uncomfortable and to my surprise stated, "Me!"

Then he informed me there seemed to be a type of armor encasing his upper chest that felt like it was holding him together and preventing him from accessing the source of this pain. I suggested that he allow it to be there and sink inside to understand it and ask it what it was doing there.

He quickly responded, "Protecting me."

Then I asked him to peek through the other side of the armor to see what it was protecting. To his astonishment he saw a little boy about three years old playing with a truck in a sand box. I encouraged him to step through the body armor and join him. When he sat down in the sand, he realized the boy was him at age three.

I then asked Nick, "What does your little guy need to tell you?"

After a few minutes Nick sadly replied, "He says that nobody will play with him because they think he is strange. He is also very sad because Dad just left Mom and he has to hold all his feelings in and toughen up to become a man."

I asked Nick, "Where does he hold all those feelings in his little body?"

Nick grimaced and pointed to his stomach. I asked, "What do those feelings look like?"

He responded slowly, "A heavy gray mass filled with ropes tied up in knots."

I inquired, "Do you have those knots inside you adult body?"

After a few minutes of reflection, Nick said, "Yes but they have multiplied over the years tying up my entire belly."

I asked, "Do these knots affect your arm in any way, shape or form?"

Nick furrowed his eyebrows and said, "No."

I knew we had to heal these knots before we continued to research the source of the pain, so I had Nick ask his little boy in the sandbox, "What do those knots need?"

He replied, "To play, be happy and drink hot chocolate with big, white, fluffy marshmallows."

Together, Nick and his little one scooped out the knots and replaced them with hot chocolate topped with large marshmallows.

Next I suggested that Nick take time to play and reconnect with his little guy to find out why people thought he was strange. After mixing sand with water and forming a row of tall, cylindrical buildings, the little guy looked up into his eyes and asked him if he could keep a secret. Then he pulled a crumpled piece of paper out of his pocket and handed it to Nick. On this paper were pencil drawings of tall, space age structures with rings around them which symbolized a force field of energy.

Nick smiled as he recalled memories of complex drawings he had made similar to this one until the age of twelve.

Little Nick explained he had built them before.

Then Nick asked, "Where did you build them?"

Little Nick pointed into the sky and said, "Up there on a planet far away. Would you like to go there and remember with me?"

At first Nick could not grasp the magnitude of the situation but after a while he acquiesced. Then he grabbed the little guy's hand and in their imagination they flew together to a planet that was shrouded in blue clouds. Slowly they descended and landed in a city full of tall, circular buildings. These structures were made out of a special metal which created an energy field that produced negative and positive ions to continuously charge and clean up the air.

The little guy said, "I want to show you inside."

He grabbed Nick's hand and pulled him through invisible doors which opened as they approached and closed without a sound after they passed through. He ran over to the wall where shiny circular platforms hovered a foot off the ground. They were light weight, two inches thick, three feet in diameter and appeared to be made out of aluminum.

Little Nick acted like he had played with them before and jumped on one saying, "Come on, let's fly to the top of the building!"

Nick walked over to the small hovering pieces of metal and kicked one with his foot. It jumped up a few feet and returned to its resting place. Then he placed one foot on the disk and pressed it down to stabilize it on the floor. When he held it level with the floor, he jumped on it, lost his balance and fell to the ground. The metal disk flipped and returned to its original position.

Little Nick laughed and told him, "Get back on and pretend it's a skate board that can fly."

He cautiously placed his large foot on the shiny disk and jumped on. It wobbled and silently moved in circles while he learned to balance on it.

Little Nick smiled and darted upwards while looking down at Nick and said, "Don't look at it. Just focus on where you want to go and let it carry you."

Nick looked up and laughed, catching on to the idea that this little flying disk could move with his intention. He relaxed and began to silently instruct the disk to move forward. Then he levitated upwards and switched his focus from the disk to his surroundings. That is when he noticed the walls of this building were completely clear and he could see out of them just like they were glass.

They explored each level of this building and met people who looked human and greeted them with smiles but never uttered a word. At first Nick thought they couldn't speak but little Nick told him to listen with his heart. After a while he could hear words float into the sides of his head and down into his chest and he knew they were communicating with telepathy.

They came to the top floor of the building where the little guy hovered eye to eye with Nick and told him, "We are supposed to build these on our planet and clean it up."

Those words felt right inside Nick but he couldn't fathom how it could be done so he asked, "How?"

Little Nick replied with confidence, "It will be created when the time comes."

Then he pointed out into space and said, "We came from that and we have the ability to create anything we choose."

Together they watched a soft loving light pour down all around them. They hovered in this light for a while remembering their divine design. Information about Nick's future came pouring into his consciousness and he described to me in detail what he would be building.

When they were fully saturated with this future memory the adult turned to the little guy and said, "Come with me and we will go back to earth and fulfill our mission."

They took each others hands and slowly returned. Then Nick placed his little guy inside his heart along with the flying disk, sand box and chocolate milk with marshmallows and promised to play with him and fulfill his destiny.

Nick opened his eyes and stared at the ceiling. The wheels in his brain were spinning while he talked about turning his attic into a drafting room to design these buildings.

I heard months later the pain subsided when he set up a drafting room in his the attic and began to draw the buildings.

Chapter 18
INTRODUCTION TO THE MEDITATION TO CREATION

⚭

The stories you have read are just a sampling of the experiences people have had when they came to my office from all over the globe to remember their soul's purpose and live it. Some arrived to discover blocks and wounds that seemed to cause serious illness and they used them as gateways to their souls. Others trusted their heart's intuitive guidance and once they were connected to their soul there was no limit to where they could go. Some explored their past lives using them as a doorway to their soul and Creation. Then they let their soul's intelligence within the force of Creation carry them into their future in this life to see themselves fulfilling their purpose.

When I look back and remember asking for my soul's purpose to be revealed to me, tears of gratitude come to my eyes. I got what I asked for and little did I know it would completely change my life. I am grateful to all my teachers who shared their knowledge with me and my clients that believed in my soul's gift. They let me share this wonderful journey with them and it changed their lives by reconnecting them to their light, love, wisdom and power. They came to understand who they really were and what they came into this life to do. Many have discovered there is no limit to their soul and tapped into their true potential to become the force of Creation.

When you do this mediation trust whatever you experience even if you fall asleep. Sometimes you need to create your reality in the dreamtime before you can accept it in this time-space continuum.

If you experience frustration in your attempt the go to Creation this may be a memory from this life or a past life that is stopping you. To uncover what impedes your progress allow yourself to focus on it with your mind to discover the beliefs that prevent you from trusting yourself. Then connect your mind to your body and search for the sensations or feelings that correspond with your thoughts. Once you locate them, sink inside and feel. Then let your emotions take you back to the memory. Take your time to uncover it and once you find it, sit in this memory to understand how it restrains you. After that, ask what it needs to be released and healed. Then use your imagination to scoop out what holds you back and replace it with what you need to be liberated. Once you free yourself, do the meditation again. Do not be surprised if you have different experiences each time that you take this journey.

When you access your ability to create in this dimension the information and energy may begin to build. As it grows your life may change and you will become a boundless, limitless being expressing the magnificence of your soul.

Take liberties to write your own meditation and go to Creation your way. There are no rules so use your method or technique to become a diverse being expressing your creativity. Trust that you are a creative, immortal being with an infinite wisdom that flows from Creation into your soul giving you an eternal intelligence with solutions to every situation in your life.

I invite you to join me and experience this journey by making an audio recording of the meditation below. To embrace the experience fully, pause at the end of each paragraph or wherever you need to take more time before moving on. When you listen to your recording make sure you are comfortable and will not be disturbed. After you have completed your journey write down what you felt, saw and/or heard and what you have come to fulfill in your lifetime.

Chapter 19

THE MEDITATION

∽

You are Creation.
This is your sacred time to return to Creation and remember who and what you have always been and will always be. You have the ability to bring the force of Creation into your body and manifest its power into your life.

Prepare for your journey to Creation by focusing on your breath. Take a long, slow, deep breath in and out while instructing your mind to follow your breath. As your mind follows your breath, let your body begin to relax.

Bring your awareness all the way down inside your feet and feel inside your feet for any tension or tightness.

Take a deep breath inside both feet and on the out breath allow all the tension and tightness to slide right out and feel both feet relaxing. There is no place to go right now. Just be right here.

Now bring your awareness up inside both legs and feel inside both legs for any holding. Take a deep breath inside both legs and on the out breath feel the holding slide right out. Let both legs drop and relax.

Slowly bring your awareness up inside your belly and tummy area. Sink your awareness deep inside and feel for any apprehension or nervousness that may lie inside there. Take a deep breath in, fully expanding your belly and tummy. And on the out breath allow any apprehension or nervousness to slide right out. Feel this entire area becoming calm and relaxed.

Now move slowly up inside your chest cavity and feel inside for any constriction or tightness. Take a big deep breath in expanding your chest cavity and on the out breath allow any constriction or tightness to slide right out. Feel your entire chest cavity softening and relaxing.

Now move up inside your shoulders and imagine two big worlds, one on each shoulder. As you feel the weight of them on your shoulders imagine them rolling right off. There is nothing to be responsible for now.

Once you let them go, sink inside your shoulders and feel for any tension. Take a big, deep breath right inside both shoulders and on the out breath feel the tension sliding right out. Let your shoulders drop and relax.

Slowly move down inside your arms and feel for any holding in your upper arm, lower arms, wrists, hands and fingers. Breathe deeply into both arms and as you breathe out allow any holding to slide right out your arms, wrists, hands and fingers. Feel both arms dropping and letting go. There is nothing to hold onto.

Now, slowly move up your arms, up into your shoulders, up into your throat and feel your throat relaxing.

Bring your awareness up inside your jaw and feel your jaw muscles relaxing.

Now move your attention around your mouth and feel around your mouth softening.

Gently move up inside your cheeks and feel your cheeks softening.

Slowly come up around your eyes and feel around your eyes softening.

Now come up inside your forehead and feel for any tension or tightness. Take a big deep breath right into your forehead and on the out breath allow the tension and tightness to slide right out. Feel your forehead relaxing.

As your forehead and your whole body completely relax bring your awareness down inside your heart. As you sink down inside your heart, once again tell your mind to follow your breath and listen to your heart.

As you sit inside your heart imagine a ball of light glowing inside the very center and illuminating your heart. Imagine it pulsing to the rhythm of your heart beat and emanating a bright and powerful light. This is the light of your soul. In a moment you will expand this ball of light all around your body to create a cocoon of protection.

Now, take a deep breath into this light and on the out breath expand this glowing, pulsing ball of light out all around you creating a cocoon of light. Use your imagination to visualize it.

Now it is time to expand this cocoon of light even further out. Take a deep breath right into this cocoon and on the out breath expand it one hundred feet out in all directions. Feel the vast magnificence of the power in this vibrating, pulsing force all around you. Visualize your cocoon filled with a luminous, silver-blue liquid light.

Now it is time to activate your spheres within your cocoon. Take a big, deep breath into your spheres and on the out breath spin them, one to the left and one to the right until their rotation synchronizes with the rhythm of your heartbeat.

It is time to fly. Feel the force within your luminous spheres of light building with intensity and beginning to lift you up...up and up...up into the sky caring you up and out into earth's atmosphere moving out through the atmosphere and out into space. Be aware of your sphere's intelligence continuing to carry you out towards Mars...moving quickly past Mars and beyond...moving even faster and powering out through the asteroid belt... on and on and on...

Powering up and speeding towards Jupiter moving quickly past Jupiter and on.....out towards Neptune...closer and closer...moving past Neptune on...continuing on and on...towards Pluto...past Pluto and on...out and out and out.

Increasing in speed now and moving out towards the Milky Way... move out through the Milky Way and beyond.

Feel your spheres building force and merging together creating a sphere of light and streaming past galaxies that appear as clusters of energy...moving quickly on and on...out and out.

Past constellations...on and on...out and out...through the infinite cosmos...and on toward the end of the universe...moving out and out...all the way out to the edge of the universe, coming right up to the edge of the universe and popping right through the embryonic wall of the universe.

Now moving out into the black void and as you move out become aware of many universes all around you. As you pass through this vast, black ocean filled with universes take time to become aware of their immensity... passing by all the universes and out deeper and deeper into the void... continuing out now and coming up to the first wall of the delineation of dimensions. As you come up to this wall allow your sphere to propel you through it and expand even more...out and out moving deeper and deeper into the darkness...moving out further and further and coming up to the second wall. Sliding right through and expanding even more and moving even deeper within the void. As you move out, feel yourself coming up to the last wall and allow your sphere to carry you right through it.

As you move out the other side, feel yourself moving out of the void and into the soft loving light of Creation. Feel yourself returning home.

Now moving gently further and further into the light...feel it enveloping you...embracing you and welcoming you...Breathe in its love and feel the peace of Creation pouring into you.

Feel its pure unconditional love and light pouring inside your body and out into your sphere. Allow its benevolent power to pour into you and reactivate your ability to create.

Now listen to the sound of Creation and its infinite wisdom pouring into you...through you...

Now that you have filled yourself with the love, light, wisdom and the power to create...it is time to return.

It is time to bring the force of Creation back with you to earth.

And now breathe this light, love, wisdom and power in and anchor it in the very center of your heart and allow your heart to become one with the force of Creation.

With this force anchored in your heart allow it to pour into every cell of your being. As it fills every cell of your being let it overflow and pour out into your sphere. Watch it filling up your sphere and powering it up to return.

Slowly begin to move out of Creation towards the void. As you slowly move out of Creation use your sphere's force field to create a path of the light through the black outer wall of the delineation of dimensions.

Let its light, wisdom, love and benevolent power pour down creating a stream of light which illuminates the darkness.

Moving down and down through the second wall and powering right through it.

Move down through the wall and laser a pathway for the light stream of Creation to pour right through the last wall...moving all the way through and into the void...down and down and down and down.

As you approach the field of universes, let yourself see all of them. Moving down and down towards the universes and begin to pass by them... feel yourself streaming down through them coming closer and closer and closer towards your universe.

Bringing the light stream of Creation down...streaming right up to the edge of your universe and taking a deep breath and on the out breath pouring the light stream right thought the embryonic wall of your universe watching it open and allowing you to return...streaming down and feeling the wall close behind you and moving into your universe. Streaming down and down towards the constellations down and down and down...towards the nebulas. Quickly passing them and on...and on...

Moving down past the clusters and on streaming down past the galaxies and see how they look moving down past all the galaxies into your universe and toward the Milky Way. Down and down...moving into the Milky Way...moving down and down and down all the way through the Milky Way towards your galaxy...closer and closer and closer...now coming into view of your galaxy...pouring your light stream right inside you galaxy.

Down and down and down...streaming down towards Pluto and past Pluto...down towards Neptune and on past Neptune...continuing down and down and down...down past Jupiter and on and on... streaming towards the Asteroid belt and down and down. Moving right into the Asteroid belt and all the way though it.

Moving down towards Mars and pouring your light stream right past Mars and coming into view of your earth...closer and closer and closer.

Moving down and down coming right down into earths atmosphere. Bringing the light stream from Creation and pouring into earth's atmosphere.

Feel the light of Creation streaming down with you...closer and closer.

As you approach your earth, feel the light of Creation streaming down into the sky and approaching your physical body...down and down...coming right down inside your physical body. Feel the light pouring down into you. Breathe it down into the top of your head, down into your body, allowing it to fill your heart with the light, wisdom, love and benevolent power of Creation reactivating your ability to create.

When it fills your body, allow it to overflow and pour out your hands into the world around you. Then allow it to pour out your feet and down into the earth filling the earth with the light of Creation.

You are now a portal of Creation. As this light pours through you and into the earth visualize yourself creating your life with the power, wisdom, love and light of Creation.

BIBLIOGRAPHY

Wanda was born in the winter of 1959 in Glendale, Arizona where her parents had a dairy farm. She was the sixth of nine children and shortly after birth, her family moved to Escondido, California where she grew up and was educated in organic gardening, herbal wild crafting, natural foods, energy therapy, alternative medicine and the love of the creator. This natural environment created a strong foundation that inspired her to seek a career in the alternative healing arts.

In 1983, she co-hosted psychic fairs and a metaphysical lecture series with her business partner, Dian Crystal, while studying privately with a teacher from the Berkeley Psychic Institute. In 1986 she became certified as a massage therapist through M.I.T. in Carmel Valley, California.

She continued her education by attending one of the largest healing schools in the country, Barbara Brennan's School of Healing, where she studied with Barbara Brennan who authored "Hands of Light" and "Light Emerging."

In addition to career training as a psychic, massage therapist and healer, Wanda studied nutrition with noted health educators: Jeffery Bland CN, Andrew Weil MD, Michael Tierra MH, Janet Zand ND, and many others.

Since 1989, Wanda has practiced Soul Transformation Sessions, Medical Intuitive Readings, Aura/Chakra Scanning, Emotional Core Wound Healing, Psychic Readings, Past Life Regressions and Future Life Progressions.

She also created the School of Medical Intuitive Mastery where she teaches people from around the globe to activate their abilities to see, hear and feel inside their bodies, its energy fields and connect with their souls to return to Creation.

Wanda lives in Sedona, Arizona and can be reached through her website: http://www.medicalintuitivemastery.com/

65334255R00060

Made in the USA
San Bernardino, CA
31 December 2017